Mennonites
in
Winnipeg

Leo Driedger

Winnipeg, MB Canada   **Kindred Press**   Hillsboro, KS USA

Canadian Cataloguing in Publication Data

Driedger, Leo
Mennonites in Winnipeg

    Bibliography: p.
    ISBN: 0-919797-96-2

1. Mennonites - Manitoba - Winnnipeg.   2. Mennonites - Manitoba - Winnipeg - History. I. Title.

<u>BX8118.7.W56D75 1989</u>   289.7'71274   C89-0980740-8

69042

MENNONITES IN WINNIPEG

Published simultaneously by Kindred Press, Winnipeg, Manitoba R2L 2E5 and Kindred Press, Hillsboro, Kansas 67063

Typesetting and design by Publishing Services, Winnipeg, MB

Cover design by Sleeping Tiger Artworks, Winnipeg,Manitoba

Printed by D.W. Friesen & Sons, Altona, Manitoba

International Standard Book Number 0-919797-96-2

Printed in Canada

MENNONITES IN WINNIPEG

PREFACE

We have been looking forward to the coming of delegates from many different countries and cultures to Winnipeg for the Mennonite World Conference. Mennonite Central Committee Manitoba (MCCM), the inter-Mennonite relief and service agency of this area, also wishes to welcome guests to this special 1990 occasion. MCCM set aside a small fund and asked me to do some research and writing as a contribution to this event. *Mennonites in Winnipeg* is the result.

Since there are more Mennonites in Winnipeg than in any city of the world, we thought guests and tourists might want to know more about us. No one has written such an introduction to Mennonites before, so this small book may well be of interest not only to Winnipeggers and others in Canada but also to those of other nationalities.

This short introduction is but a beginning. Much more research is needed. I wish to thank the many individuals from churches, educational institutions, businesses, service agencies, the communications field and arts community who were willing to provide interviews and information. Thanks also to Victor Doerksen, Diane Driedger, Henry Dueck, David Duerksen, Adolf Ens, John Friesen, Ben and Esther Horch who read the manuscript and made helpful comments, and to Darlene Driedger who typed several drafts. Special thanks to the Mennonite World Conference which provided a grant to publish this book, making it available at the convention at a subsidized price. It was a pleasure to work with Gilbert Brandt and Kindred Press in the production of this book.

Leo Driedger
University of Manitoba
Winnipeg, 1990

INTRODUCTION

For centuries Amsterdam was the largest Mennonite urban center, but this has changed. The 19,105 Mennonites located in metropolitan Winnipeg represent an adult membership of 9,350 baptized believers who worship in forty-seven churches throughout the city. In this short volume we wish to introduce you to Winnipeg Mennonites. How did they first come to the city? How do they live today and what institutions have they built?

Early Beginnings

The aboriginals used the Fort Garry area as a fishing and hunting base for centuries. Between 1670 and 1870 it was a major fur trading center. The Saulteaux Indians and Métis had begun to gather at the Forks in the early 1800s, and after 1821 retired Hudson's Bay Company officers and their families settled in large numbers in this area.

The province of Manitoba (1870) and Winnipeg city (1874) are little more than one hundred years old. The first Mennonites to set foot on Winnipeg soil were the delegates from Russia who came to find land in 1873. In the first seven chapters we trace the early history of the Fort Garry area, the beginnings of Mennonite missions in North End Winnipeg, the coming of Russian Mennonites in the 1920s and their village settlement in what is now North Kildonan. We trace how Elmwood became a Mennonite Brethren institutional center, how the traditional rural Kanadier Mennonites came to Winnipeg much later in the 1950s, and finally how Mennonites spread from several North End, West End and North Kildonan nuclei to the entire city by the 1980s.

The Social Setting Today

Winnipeg is a metropolis with a population well over 650,000 people. Distinct regions used to be independent until the metropolis became one of the first politically integrated unicity governments on the continent. Many of these areas have their own histories which are still ongoing, and Mennonites have been more a part of some regions than others. As il-

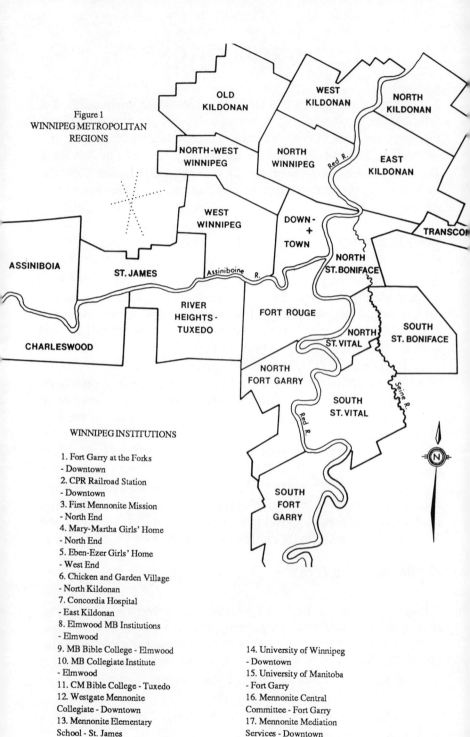

Figure 1
WINNIPEG METROPOLITAN
REGIONS

OLD KILDONAN

WEST KILDONAN

NORTH KILDONAN

NORTH-WEST WINNIPEG

NORTH WINNIPEG

EAST KILDONAN

Red R.

WEST WINNIPEG

DOWN- + TOWN

NORTH ST. BONIFACE

TRANSCON

ASSINIBOIA

ST. JAMES

Assiniboine R.

RIVER HEIGHTS - TUXEDO

FORT ROUGE

NORTH ST. VITAL

SOUTH ST. BONIFACE

CHARLESWOOD

NORTH FORT GARRY

SOUTH ST. VITAL

Seine R.

Red R.

SOUTH FORT GARRY

N

WINNIPEG INSTITUTIONS

1. Fort Garry at the Forks
- Downtown
2. CPR Railroad Station
- Downtown
3. First Mennonite Mission
- North End
4. Mary-Martha Girls' Home
- North End
5. Eben-Ezer Girls' Home
- West End
6. Chicken and Garden Village
- North Kildonan
7. Concordia Hospital
- East Kildonan
8. Elmwood MB Institutions
- Elmwood
9. MB Bible College - Elmwood
10. MB Collegiate Institute
- Elmwood
11. CM Bible College - Tuxedo
12. Westgate Mennonite
Collegiate - Downtown
13. Mennonite Elementary
School - St. James

14. University of Winnipeg
- Downtown
15. University of Manitoba
- Fort Garry
16. Mennonite Central
Committee - Fort Garry
17. Mennonite Mediation
Services - Downtown

lustrated in Figure 1, Mennonites first settled in the North End by establishing a mission shortly after the turn of the century. During the 1920s they settled in the West End and North Kildonan. These areas have become strong Mennonite communities.

It was only after World War II that Mennonites began to shift from their original territory, from the more heterogeneous religious and ethnic areas north of the Assiniboine River, to the predominantly Anglo-Saxon southern part of the city. While churches, schools and businesses were set up in the central and northern half of Winnipeg, after the 1940s the Mennonite Diaspora to the suburbs and areas south of the Assiniboine (Fort Rouge, Fort Garry, St. Vital, Tuxedo) began in earnest. Now forty-seven Mennonite churches are scattered all over the metropolitan area.

Places of Worship

Mennonites originated as a distinct religious group during the Reformation and the forty-seven Mennonite churches clearly symbolize the religious importance of the Anabaptist movement. With a few exceptions Winnipeg Mennonites represent the Anabaptists of northern Europe who had their roots in the Netherlands and trekked eastward to Prussia and Russia before coming to Canada. There are hardly any Swiss Mennonites in Winnipeg (they settled mainly in eastern North America), so those Russian Mennonites who came in the 1870s, 1920s and 1950s represent the two largest General Conference Mennonite and Mennonite Brethren Conference groups who settled in western Canada. The Mennonite Brethren began mission work largely with Germans in the North End in the 1910s, but it was the second wave of Russian immigrants in the 1920s which accelerated the growth of the Mennonite presence in Winnipeg.

About one-third of the Winnipeg Mennonites are General Conference, another third are Mennonite Brethren, and the remaining third represents numerous groups including the Evangelical Mennonite (EMC), Evangelical Mennonite Mission (EMMC), Evangelical Mennonite Brethren (EMB) and Sommerfelder conferences. Two major clusters of churches are located in the earlier settlements within the West End and North Kildonan, and the rest are scattered throughout the metropolitan region. These churches range in size from twelve to 1,400 members; their buildings vary enormously in both size and sophistication, and the age of these churches ranges from a few years to seventy-five years.

Making a Living

In chapters 8-14 we describe how Mennonites in the city make a living. They have built institutions such as hospitals, senior citizens' homes and schools, and are engaged in radio, television, music and the literary arts. Winnipeg Mennonites have entered most of the professions. Two popular professions are the teaching and medical services with hundreds of individuals involved at all levels. There are well over 1,000 Mennonites in business heading some of the largest companies, especially in building, furniture manufacturing, retailing and transportation. Winnipeg Mennonites appear daily on radio and TV news. They have also entered politics at all levels and are represented in the provincial cabinet and federal government.

Preparation for Life

While most children of Winnipeg Mennonites attend the public schools and hundreds of adults are in the teaching profession, some send their children to Mennonite Elementary School which opened in 1982. Two Mennonite high schools and two colleges opened after the mid-1940s. It is possible for a child to attend a Mennonite school from kindergarten through college, thereby being exposed mainly to Mennonite teachers. Some choose to send their children to both the private and public schools throughout the various levels. The five Mennonite schools teach more than 1,300 students, a majority of them being of Mennonite background.

Creative Communication

Winnipeg has become the center of Mennonite communications through newspapers, radio, television, music, the literary arts and drama. *Die Mennonitische Rundschau*, one of the oldest Mennonite papers in North America, first came to Winnipeg in 1923 and has since been published here for more than sixty-five years. A dozen Mennonite newspapers have or had their editorial offices in Winnipeg, making it a major center of the news media. There are two Mennonite book publishers and two Mennonite communication centers, established over fifty years ago, produce, distribute and broadcast religious radio and television programs.

Winnipeg has always been a center for music making with its annual music competition and festival. Mennonites have played an important role in music appreciation. Some of the well-known Mennonite conductors have been and still are located in the city. Annual musical performances, festivals, workshops, orchestras, choirs and soloists continue to emanate especially from the two Mennonite colleges and the University of Manitoba.

While early writers and poets sought to bridge the gap between their lost homeland in Russia and their new Canadian pioneer life, recent literary writers, poets and artists are trying to deal with cultural discontinuities. The clash between rural traditional Mennonite life and the new demands of the city are more easily integrated by some Mennonites than others. Dozens of writers and poets are at the edge of this literary flowering in Winnipeg.

Relating to Others

Many of the older Mennonites in Winnipeg received help from the Mennonite Central Committee in Russia in the 1920s. Others served in alternative service in the 1940s during World War II and were exposed to the needs of a larger society. MCC Canada and MCC Manitoba have found an empathetic and permanent home in Winnipeg with its central offices located here since 1964. These two agencies have spawned numerous other related social services in the name of Christ. The interchurch Foodgrains Bank, relief and material aid centers, thrift shops, self-help crafts, offender ministries, services to aboriginals, mediation services, Mennonite Economic Development Associates (MEDA) office, and centers for inner city family services are some examples. The Mennonite churches also have their local outreach programs involving camps, retreats, evangelism, agape kitchens, etc.

This is but a short outline of some of the topics discussed in this book. We hope you will find this sketch of Mennonite beginnings interesting. For those who wish to visit some of these places of worship, life and work, we trust this introduction will be useful.

1

FORT GARRY AT THE FORKS

When the first Mennonite immigrants to Manitoba arrived on the river-boat *International* on July 31, 1874, they stopped at "The Forks," the junction of the Red and Assiniboine rivers, in the heart of present-day Winnipeg. Five boatloads of Mennonites arrived in July and September of 1874, but some stopped only to purchase supplies before they continued on to disembark at the forks of the Red and Rat rivers thirty kilometers south, now Ste. Agathe.[1] These early conservative Mennonites wanted to farm, not settle in the city. What did they see when they stopped briefly at the Forks in 1874?

The Fort at the Forks

The Hudson's Bay Company (HBC) was granted the vast territory of the Canadian northwest between the Great Lakes and the Rockies, where its employees traded for furs with the Indians for 200 years between 1670 and 1870. The Bay store on Portage Avenue continues to do business in Winnipeg today.[2] The HBC and its main competitor, the North West Company from Montreal, established forts throughout the Northwest to trade European goods for furs. As many as five different forts had been located at and around the forks of the Red and Assiniboine rivers during one time or another. The stone fort which the Mennonites saw (its turret is showing on photo 1), was built in 1835, replacing several of the forts built earlier.[3] Upper Fort Garry, as it was called, was demolished and now only the north gate remains, located between the Canadian National Railway station and the Fort Garry Hotel. However, another similar stone fort, Lower Fort Garry, is still intact and open to visitors. It is situated along the Red River, thirty kilometers north of Winnipeg.

Upper Fort Garry was the focal point of activity at the Forks when the fur trade was dominant. However, in 1812 Lord Selkirk brought over a group of Scottish settlers who began farming a kilometer north of the Forks area on the west side of the Red River. These Selkirk settlers were the first white agriculturalists in western Canada. The HBC fur traders, the Indians who brought furs to be sold, and the Métis who made their livelihood as transporters and suppliers, were not happy to see the agriculturalists. However, the Selkirk Settlement did not survive.

Four years before the Mennonites came, Louis Riel, a Métis leader captured Upper Fort Garry and set up a provisional government, seeking provincial recognition from Ottawa. But the military was sent from the East, Riel was forced to flee, and Manitoba did become the fifth province of Canada in 1870.[4] A monument on the legislative grounds honors Louis Riel as the father of Manitoba. The Mennonites who saw the same fort in 1874 were among the first permanent agricultural settlers who began the East (around Steinbach) and West (around Winkler) reserves, fifty kilometers southeast and one hundred kilometers south of Winnipeg respectively. Agriculture had permanently invaded the region where until 1870 fur had been dominant.

1874 Arrival of the First Mennonites at Fort Garry.

Winnipeg: Muddy Waters

The junction of the Red and Assiniboine rivers had been known throughout the fur-trading community as "The Forks" long before the competing fur-trade companies built their forts. There were relatively few people settled around the area, but slowly a permanent population grew, so ox cart trails began to develop, linking the many trading forts. The main thoroughfares of Portage Avenue and Main Street in Winnipeg today were originally cart trails. The name "Winnipeg" was first used by the *Nor'wester* newspaper on February 24, 1866. The previous issues of this paper had carried the designation "Red River Settlement, Assiniboia", on its masthead.[5] Winnipeg is a Cree name given to the lake fifty-five kilometers north, meaning muddy ("win") and water ("nippee"). By 1870 the town of Winnipeg was shown on maps of the area even though it was not incorporated. It officially became a city in November 1873 and its council first met in January 1874.[6] The population grew so fast, it skipped incorporation as a village or town.

When the area became the province of Manitoba in 1870, demands for merchandise, lumber, agricultural implements and land increased so Winnipeg grew from a small population of one hundred in 1870 to 3,700 by 1874.[7] When one group of Mennonites stopped briefly in 1874 to buy shovels, scythes, hayforks, stoves, coffee mills, frying pans, wagons, horses, cattle, flour and other provisions, Winnipeg was on the verge of an economic boom.[8] By the end of 1873 Winnipeg had more than 900 buildings, including over one hundred mercantile concerns, twenty-seven manufacturing industries, plus offices, hotels and dwellings.[9] Although the size of population suggests an urban area, qualitatively it was a cow town because "it was without sidewalks or pavements; it had neither waterworks, sewage nor street lights. The nearest railroad was south in Moorhead on the Red River, 222 miles away. Its connection with the outer world was one, or possibly two steamers on the Red River in summer."[10] It was also 2,200 kilometers from Ottawa without any transport connections with the rest of Canada.

Rural Mennonite Reserves

"A brief period of five years between 1873 and 1878 witnessed the mass exodus of 15,000, or 30 percent of the total Mennonite population in the Ukraine to Canada and the United States."[11] When the Mennonites left the Russian Ukraine in the 1870s, the group parted ways in North America. A large number settled on the American prairies, chiefly Kansas, and another large group came to Manitoba. "In a short space of three years, 1,200 . . . households comprising 6,140 souls were transplanted from their villages in southern Russia to the virgin soil of Manitoba between 1874 and 1876."[12] It was the more conservative Mennonites from Chortitza, Bergthal and the Kleine Gemeinde who settled in the two reserves designated exclusively for Mennonites. None of these early Mennonites stayed in Winnipeg. It was only after World War II, seventy years later, that many of the grandchildren of these early immigrants began to migrate to Winnipeg.

The two reserves of land are referred to even today as the East Reserve and West Reserve. A total of fifty-nine villages were established on the East Reserve located between Niverville and Steinbach, including Kleine Gemeinde and Bergthaler (most of whom later moved to the West Reserve). The village of Steinbach, sixty kilometers southeast of Winnipeg, has since developed into a small city of 8,390 in 1981, more than twice the size of Winnipeg in 1874. The large Mennonite Village Museum located there shows the "simlin" in which some early settlers spent their first winter, as well as the house-barn combinations they built. Many of these settlers were the less well-to-do and many had been landless in Russia, so they began in a difficult situation. Since the land in the East Reserve tended to be sandy, stony and poorly drained, many soon went into mixed farming, including animal husbandry. The Kleine Gemeinde, now called the Evangelical Mennonite Conference (EMC), moved to Winnipeg only after World War II and did not establish churches there until the late 1950s.

The West Reserve was established by Reinländer, often called Old Colony, and Bergthaler Mennonites on the west side of the Red River near the American border about one hundred kilometers south of Winnipeg. They established seventy villages, churches and schools.[13] The 3,240 Old Colony Mennonites who began coming in 1875 were the most conservative and have not yet established a church in Winnipeg. They perceived the city as a threat to their survival. Large numbers moved to Mexico in the 1920s because of the encroachment of "the world" upon their communities. The West Reserve is located between Altona and Morden, with Winkler being the largest Mennonite community (population 6,538 in 1981) located in the heart of the reserve. The Bergthaler, although not as conservative as the Old Colony, did not establish a church in Winnipeg until 1957.

We have briefly reviewed the coming of the early Mennonites to rural Manitoba to provide the social context for later migration into the city. The early southern rural Mennonites remained in rural Manitoba; they did not spearhead the influx of Mennonites to Winnipeg. They came later in the 1950s when others had already lived there and had built their institutions for forty years. Who then lead the beginnings of the greatest urban Mennonite concentration ever? While early rural Mennonites have contributed to the Winnipeg expansion for the last thirty-five years, it was the Russian Mennonites coming to Manitoba fifty years later in the 1920s who began the urban explosion. We need to trace their beginnings in Winnipeg.

Canadian Pacific Railway Station where Mennonites of the 1920s arrived in Winnipeg. (Photo: Leo Driedger)

2

BEGINNINGS IN THE WINNIPEG
NORTH END

Winnipeg's North End is probably the best known district in the city, its name signifying a good deal more than its geography. "North End was synonymous with the 'Foreign Quarter,' 'New Jerusalem,' and 'CPR Town.'"[1] Let us explain what was meant, because it was in this area of the city the Mennonites began their mission work.

The North End "Foreign Quarter"

The first transcontinental Canadian Pacific Railway (CPR) came into this city in 1885, separating the northern part of the city from the central and southern parts. Between 1882 and 1884 the CPR built its yards, shops and roundhouse just north of the center of the city, and these were enlarged after 1903 to become the "largest railway yards in the world." The huge CPR facilities were the major industry in the North End, dominating the area with a maze of buildings and tracks, noise, dirt and smell. Winnipeg became a major railway center, and by 1911 3,500 workers were employed by the CPR.[2]

Many of these CPR workers lived in the North End within walking distance, creating a large working class neighborhood, thus the designation "CPR Town." City developers also encouraged the character of the North End as a working class and immigrant area by building small cheap houses on small lots north of the tracks. Thus the area became a high density area, with little diversity in housing shapes and sizes, and no open spaces for parks or recreation. The spatial layout and structure determined a lower class neighborhood.

The North End was therefore labeled the "Foreign Quarter" and lower working class area, which to this day has remained an ethnically plural sub-society. Eastern Europeans, especially Jews, Ukrainians, Poles and Germans, many of whom also came from Russia and Poland, settled here. While the North End has always been segregated from the southern, more Anglo-Saxon parts of Winnipeg, the railroad assured its spatial and social segregation as hundreds of freight trains choked the tracks blocking traffic to the North End. Even the streetcars often did not cross the maze of tracks so transfers were necessary at limited points of crossing. By 1914 only two overhead bridges and two subways provided access to the North End.

Even politically, Winnipeg is still a divided city, with northern Winnipeg voting for the New Democratic Party (NDP) and the Anglo-Saxon better-to-do south voting Conservative. In 1916 eighty percent of the city's Jews and Slavs, sixty-seven percent of the Scandinavians and twenty-two percent of the Germans were located in the North End.[3] There were twelve Jewish synagogues in the North End in 1912 and many foreign language newspapers and institutions. The Ukrainians published at least five newspapers and supported active clubs and societies as well. In 1905 the Aberdeen and Strathcona schools in Wards 5 and 6 of the North End included almost exclusively children of British origin (ninety-eight and ninety-five percent); by 1915 they had declined to seventeen and eight percent, while Jewish students had increased to sixty-seven percent and forty-three percent respectively. About one-fifth of the students in Strathcona in 1915 were Ukrainian and another fifth German. The North End had indeed become a "foreign quarter." It was in this setting the first Mennonites began to work.

Early Mennonite Missions

Several Mennonite families and German Baptists from Russia began to meet in homes in the North End as early as 1907.[4] Some Mennonites joined the German Baptist Church but others contacted the Mennonite

Brethren in Winkler (in the West Reserve) to serve them in Winnipeg. Several leaders came to meet with them, and soon they "bought an empty lot at the corner of Burrows and Andrews, bought a small chapel which was moved from St. Vital onto this lot and so the Sunday services began."[5] On November 1, 1913 Rev. and Mrs. W.J. Bestvater of Mountain Lake, Minnesota came as the first Mennonite Brethren missionaries and began the work with twenty-two members. The Winkler brethren had baptized some, but only one family of Mennonite background was included in the membership. This was to be a mission to the large numbers of German Lutherans, Baptists and some Mennonites in the North End.

In 1914, a year later, it became necessary to have larger premises, so they rented a mission chapel on Manitoba and McKenzie from the German Baptists where they worshiped until 1917.[6] This was during the First World War years, so Bestvater also had to help some young Mennonite men with their military exemptions. It was a poor area, people were very transient, and immigrants were coming and going; people needed a great deal of help spiritually, physically and socially. Additional assistance became necessary, so on December 1, 1915 Anna Thiessen, a young Saskatchewan woman just out of school, arrived as the second missionary. It was into this setting that the Lutheran Edward Horch family (parents of the well-known musician Ben Horch) came to the Mennonite church.[7]

In 1917 the congregation moved from McKenzie and Manitoba into the basement of a new mission hall which the Mennonite Brethren built on the same corner of Burrows and Andrews that their former little chapel of 1913 had been. They named it North End Chapel and worshiped there until 1930. The congregation had grown and needed permanent space, but the intended upper portion of the church was never built. Today it is a sausage factory and the stone basement chapel with a temporary roof still exists. In 1917 the war was not yet over, and their German services and Saturday German language school attracted attention. Children threw stones and sometimes policemen harassed them. By 1921 there were fifty-nine members in the church and many non-members always attended so the chapel was usually filled.[8]

In 1923 Russian Mennonite immigrants began coming to Winnipeg in large numbers. After many hardships during the Russian

Revolution of 1917, many Mennonite Brethren also came to the North End and the stone basement chapel again became too small. In 1930 they built a much larger 500 seat church at 621 College Avenue where the congregation met until 1954. This influx of more educated German-speaking Russian Mennonites tended to swamp the little North End Chapel of German Lutheran background Mennonites, so many German Lutherans left. Thus the North End MB Church became one of predominantly recent Russian immigrant stock, which continued German services in its new facilities. In 1954 this congregation moved east across the Red River to Elmwood, where they now worship in a larger brick church. The old stucco College Avenue church still exists and is used by the Winnipeg Christian Reformed Church.

3

THE RUSSIAN MENNONITE INVASION

The mission program in the Winnipeg North End was directed largely to Germans of non-Mennonite background, supported by a few Mennonite families. By 1921 this had resulted in a small cluster of fifty-nine members in one small basement church. While the first Mennonite immigrants who came to rural Manitoba in the 1870s did not migrate to the city, this second migration who came to the prairies in the 1920s were more open to settlement in the city because they had grown accustomed to industrialization in Russia in the fifty year interval. Their economic state, along with the Depression of the 1930s, sent a wave of these recent immigrants to various cities. This substantial influx greatly changed and boosted Mennonite numbers in Winnipeg.

Russian Immigrant Needs and Services

The Russian Mennonites who began coming to Canada in 1923 went mainly to the western prairies, and they had to funnel by rail through Winnipeg, the gateway to the west. Winnipeg was an important stop, since they had been on the transcontinental CPR train for days, coming from Quebec City and Montreal after transferring from ships which carried them across the Atlantic. These Mennonite immigrants came by the thousands, having lived through the Russian Revolution. Lots of them had lost everything and many others had lived through famine, so they were poor and destitute.

The CPR railroad station, built in 1904, still exists on Higgins Avenue south of the tracks, although it is no longer used as a passenger depot. Jewish, Ukrainian and Polish East European immigrants had arrived at the station earlier, so it became a landmark for those living in the North End and West End. An Immigration Hall (removed in the 1970s) to the east of the CPR station was an important stop-off for those coming west. Soon C.N. and Tina Hiebert, who came in 1925 as the new missionaries for the North End Chapel, spent a great deal of their time serving these newly-arrived Russian immigrants.[1] Hiebert often visited the Immigration Hall at the CPR station, walking through the trains which stopped for several hours or longer on their way west. Sometimes evening services were held in the hall; other times Hiebert read some scripture and prayed with the immigrants who sat on their suitcases.

Since newly-arrived immigrants were not supposed to be a burden to the city, those who became ill were dependent on help, which the Hieberts and Anna Thiessen freely gave. Many stayed overnight. The Hieberts and Thiessen helped these immigrants to adjust, and since many new Mennonites could not speak English, there was much need for interpretation. In 1926 the membership of North End Chapel nearly doubled because of the influx of immigrants. Once again the building was too small.[2] This chapel was the only Mennonite church in Winnipeg and it was always filled. In fact, Hiebert spent so much time with the newly-arrived immigrants, his mission board sought ways to relieve him of the double burden. More resources were needed, which lead to the establishment of the Mennonite Girls' Homes, another interesting part of Mennonite urban beginnings in Winnipeg.

Mennonite Girls' Homes

The beginning of the Mennonite Girls' Homes is important in the development of a Mennonite presence in Winnipeg. Some of the single Russian women who arrived at the Immigration Hall after 1923 immediately looked for jobs; some began working as maids for the wealthy families of the city.[3] Since many of these new arrivals were poor, having lost everything during the Russian Revolution, they also were in debt to the Canadian Pacific Railway for their travel to Canada (the debt was called *Reiseschuld*). Some of the young women were encouraged to find jobs to first pay their own travel debt, and then help pay the debts of others in the family. Most immigrant Mennonite families rented or bought farms, but it was difficult to start with inadequate funds, and when the Depression came after the crash of 1929, survival on the farm was almost impossible.

It is ironic that many Mennonites who used to look upon the city as evil or dangerous had to watch their young women (many in their teens) work in a large city for the "English" because of economic pressures. Most of these young women did not know English, they had to adjust to a new country and culture, and they entered family contexts where they would not see their own families for months. These young women in the city were exposed to risks, as most of them had known only their Mennonite village enclaves in Russia.[4] Entering the servant role in a new country with limited family and community support was a very difficult assignment.

While the Mennonite missionaries in the North End tried to extend their mission work to include the new immigrants, their facilities and time were severely taxed. The Hieberts kept people in their home every night but the situation demanded rearrangements. "Their hearts were filled with compassion, especially for the often perplexed parents who had to leave their inexperienced daughters behind to work in a strange city."[5] Employers were quick to get the cheapest help possible; advocates were clearly needed. At that time there were no labor relations boards, so the missionaries tried to help where they could.

By 1925 Anna Thiessen began taking in some of these girls in her two upstairs rooms at 608 Mountain Avenue. She added rented rooms to house these young women while they looked for jobs; these rooms were always overcrowded. The young women themselves began to call their facilities "Mädchenheim," or Girls' Home. Increasingly Thiessen got into job mediation, and she and the young women began to worship together.[6] By 1927 they were able to rent the bottom floor of the home so they now had seven rooms. The Mennonite Brethren conference sent Sarah Warkentin to assist Thiessen. By now the home had been named the Mary-Martha Girls' Home.

The Mountain Avenue home was soon too small, so the group moved to a larger place at 413 Boyd Avenue in 1928. By 1929 they shifted to 398 Mountain Avenue, and in 1931 they moved into a fourth home at 437 Mountain Avenue, where it stayed until the home closed in 1959. The last three places are still in existence.

A second Girls' Home was started by General Conference Mennonites in the central part of the city (south of the CPR tracks) in 1926. It was called the Eben Ezer Girls' Home, run by Helen and Neta Epp for twenty-seven years.[7] It also continued until 1959 when the need had declined. Its purpose was the same, to support young Mennonite women in the city and help them find jobs. The first Eben Ezer Home was located in rented quarters at 458 McDermot, then moved to 810 Alexander Avenue for a brief period where the church could be used for meetings, moved again to 412 Bannatyne, and finally in 1943 moved to 605 Bannatyne where it functioned until its closing.[8] Three of the four former houses used still exist. The economic and social needs changed, so there was less need for these facilities.

These Girls' Homes each served more than 1,000 young women during their tenure from 1925 through 1959, a span of almost thirty-five years. Many of the young women who worked in Winnipeg and came to worship and socialize in these homes are still alive. A number have been interviewed and they have many stories to tell . These early years in the city of Winnipeg added greatly to the urban experience of thousands of Mennonites, who either stayed in the city or later moved to it. These young women also supported the developing churches by attending them, singing in choirs and performing many services. The Girls' Homes became important social centers, which boosted the establishment of Mennonites in Winnipeg, an important part of the urbanization process.[9]

The West End of Central Winnipeg

The North End where the Mennonites first began their mission work was designated the "Foreign Quarter" by Winnipeggers, or the other side of the tracks. By 1954 most of the early Mennonites had moved out of the area. The second part of Mennonite beginnings took place on the south side of the CPR railroad, which was usually considered an Anglo-Saxon area. It was still regarded as part of central Winnipeg and referred to as the West End. It was about a twenty minute walk from downtown. Although the lots close to the south side of the railroad were also small, they soon became larger going south away from the tracks into much larger homes and into some of the better sections of the city during the 1920s.

In 1923 *Die Mennonitische Rundschau* was transferred from Scottdale, Pennsylvania to Winnipeg. It located in the West End at 672 Arlington Avenue. One year previous the magazine already was giving priority to the needs of immigrants from Russia, and several special issues were devoted to their coming, the migrations and how to find relatives in Canada.[10] Many of the Russian Mennonites who arrived in Winnipeg in 1923 also settled in the West End where *Die Rundschau* was located. By 1925 they began to meet in the afternoon for worship in the Zionskirche of the Reformed Church located at 392 Alexander Avenue, which they soon purchased.[11] Soon the church became affiliated with the Schönwieser Gemeinde, a part of a larger cluster of rural and urban congregations.

The Schönwieser, who started in 1925, stayed in the West End and have now become the First Mennonite Church located at 922 Notre Dame. It is the largest General Conference Mennonite Church in North America with 1,400 members, and also the largest Mennonite congregation in Winnipeg. While it is made up almost entirely of Russian Mennonites from the 1920s, large numbers of immigrants who came in the 1950s also worship there now. This large congregation has built its own homes for the elderly around the church, called Sunset House and Arlington Senior Citizens House at 880 Arlington.

Instead of moving out of the West End, more Mennonites have moved in since. In 1936 some Mennonite Brethren settled on Ross Avenue, and in 1940 purchased a large Wesleyan church at 520 William Avenue where a congregation of 200 still worship. They were previously referred to as the Southend MB Church (now Central MB) because they had moved south of the tracks from the North End. Since then the larger segment of this congregation has moved to the Portage Avenue MB Church. A small Spanish Christian congregation also meets in this building. In 1949 the MBs from Elmwood purchased a Baptist church at 406 Logan which became the Gospel Light Mission, an outreach project to non-Mennonites.[12] This congregation has since moved to become the Salem MB Church at 691 Alexander, which today serves the Portuguese community. Another group migrated in 1963 to become the Fort Garry MB Church located at 1771 Pembina Highway. An MB outreach program also has been developed by the Cornerstone Christian Fellowship at 700 Notre Dame Avenue, started in 1977. The Mennonite Brethren especially have begun several outreach programs in the West End, leading to the establishment of the Brooklands and Westwood churches.

In addition to the two types of Russian Mennonites (GCs and MBs) located in the West End, there are two more groups who need a comment. After the Second World War, large numbers of Mennonites again came to Canada, representing a third wave of immigrants. One group began to meet at the Canadian Mennonite Bible College for worship in 1949 and moved into their first church on Sargent and Furby in 1951. Today the Sargent Avenue Mennonite Church houses a large congregation located at 926 Garfield and Sargent, into which they moved during 1960. They represent the most recent Russian Mennonite immigrants. The Home Street Mennonite Church (318 Home) represents a fourth group (the Bergthaler) which we shall discuss later under the coming of the 1870s Kanadier.

The West End is a second important area of Winnipeg into which Mennonites moved. Unlike the North End, which most early Mennonites left, ten Mennonite churches are still located here. They represent a variety of Russian Mennonites from both the 1920s and 1950s, largely MBs and GCs, as well as *Kanadier* Mennonites who came to Manitoba early, but settled in Winnipeg later. However, in the late 1920s, a third important Mennonite center of Russian and later South American Mennonites developed to which we turn next.

4

RURBAN VILLAGE IN
NORTH KILDONAN

The third major cluster of Mennonites settled in North Kildonan in 1928. A cairn at the corner of Henderson and Edison was raised in 1978 to commemorate fifty years of Mennonite settlement. Like the settlement in the West End, this comprised mostly Russian Mennonites who came in the 1920s, and settled in North Kildonan somewhat later. Some had tried farming elsewhere but things did not work out well, so they came to this area.

The rural municipality of North Kildonan was established in 1924 in the northeast portion of Winnipeg on the east side of the Red River and amalgamated into the city in 1971.[1] Kildonan was named after the parish of Kildonan in Scotland by the Selkirk Settlers who arrived in 1812. While they settled on the west side of the river, they used the heavily wooded east side (now North Kildonan) for their wood supply. Some of their ancestors moved into North Kildonan later and some of the streets are named after them; for instance, McKay, McLeod, Pritchard, Henderson and McIvor. At the time all of the present day Kildonans (West, Old, East and North) were part of the Scottish parish of Kildonan on both sides of the Red River. Later Dutch and Ukrainian settlers also arrived.

The "Chicken and Garden Village"

F.F. Isaak and Jacob J. Neufeld, two Mennonite land agents, tried to find a larger block of land near Winnipeg where some of the Mennonites could continue to do some small farming to supply the city with garden and dairy produce. They found a twenty acre piece of land which they purchased from Wilson and Company in 1927.[2] The twenty acres were divided into large building lots so that by 1928 Mennonites such as Kornelson, Isaak, Neufeld, Friesen, Langemann, Klassen, Wittenberg, Enns, Toews, Siemens and Spenst began to build. Eight chicken barns were built on what is now Edison Avenue, stretching a kilometer east along Edison from Kildonan Road (now Henderson Highway).[3] Figure 2 shows sixteen of the original lots and their owners located along Edison.

The Mennonites who moved to the "Chicken and Garden Village," as it was called, were poor. Many built a chicken barn first and lived in it until they could afford to build a house while they worked in the city to earn some money. A.C. Defehr built a chicken barn on Henderson Highway, which was eventually moved to 233 Kingsford and can be seen today as a reconditioned house.[4] A replica of the chicken barn of A.A. DeFehr is displayed at Palliser Furniture at 55 Vulcan, which DeFehr later turned into a small woodmaking factory which has since become one of the largest factories of its kind in Canada (Palliser Furniture).

In 1929 there were nineteen families in North Kildonan. By 1933 the number had increased to forty-nine families and in 1938 the settlement had grown to ninety-two family units. By 1953 North Kildonan had 1,450 Mennonite inhabitants; in 1978 the count was between 5,500 and 6,000 people.[5] North Kildonan is the closest to a rurban (both rural and urban-like) Mennonite reserve. At first it was detached but close to the city, but it soon became a suburb as Winnipeg grew to include the area in its boundaries. In 1928 this "Chicken and Garden Village" was two kilometers north of the city, located in a wooded area which had to be cleared. Today there is little evidence of this small farm community except that many Mennonites still live in the area. Only the cairn erected on the corner of Henderson and Edison marks the place of these beginnings as do a few early buildings, most of them greatly changed.

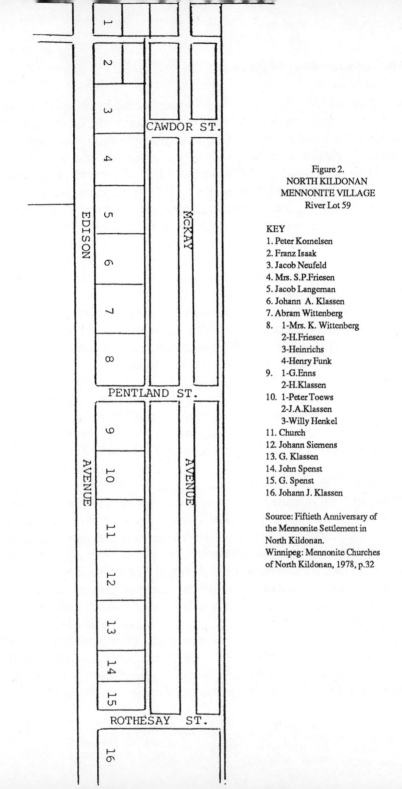

Figure 2.
NORTH KILDONAN
MENNONITE VILLAGE
River Lot 59

KEY
1. Peter Kornelsen
2. Franz Isaak
3. Jacob Neufeld
4. Mrs. S.P.Friesen
5. Jacob Langeman
6. Johann A. Klassen
7. Abram Wittenberg
8. 1-Mrs. K. Wittenberg
   2-H.Friesen
   3-Heinrichs
   4-Henry Funk
9. 1-G.Enns
   2-H.Klassen
10. 1-Peter Toews
    2-J.A.Klassen
    3-Willy Henkel
11. Church
12. Johann Siemens
13. G. Klassen
14. John Spenst
15. G. Spenst
16. Johann J. Klassen

Source: Fiftieth Anniversary of
the Mennonite Settlement in
North Kildonan.
Winnipeg: Mennonite Churches
of North Kildonan, 1978, p.32

When the Mennonites arrived in 1928, their first task was to clear the land because it was heavily wooded. Early pictures show the area to be bleak and desolate. The few roads were muddy and difficult to negotiate in spring and during the rain. Henderson Highway was not constructed until 1932. The Red River could be crossed only over the Redwood Bridge nearby and the Louise Bridge located a few kilometers to the south. Stores, schools and community facilities were sparse. The major center of social interaction was the church.[6] Let us briefly review the development of these Mennonite churches in North Kildonan.

Cluster of Mennonite Churches

A small group of about thirty Mennonite Brethren began meeting in homes in North Kildonan as soon as they arrived in 1928. Some had worshiped at the North End MB Church earlier. One year later General Conference Mennonites also settled on Devon Avenue.[7] The two MB and GC groups met together for worship in the small Mennonite Brethren church built on Edison Avenue from 1929 until 1935. Today there are nine Mennonite churches in North Kildonan clustering within a few kilometers of each other: four Mennonite Brethren and five General Conference. One of the major catalysts in church growth has been the large influx of Mennonite immigrants from South America recently.

The Mennonite Brethren who moved into their first building on Edison actually extended their original building five times before the congregation moved into larger facilities in 1957.[8] Space again became too small, so the congregation moved into the present North Kildonan MB Church building located at 217 Kingsford Avenue. The 1988 membership was 546, but some of the members have established new churches east and north of the mother church.

The North Kildonan MB congregation began Sunday school outreach farther east in a school, which led to the formation of the River East Mennonite Brethren Church on 755 McLeod Avenue in 1964, with a 1988 membership of 354. The McIvor MB Church also has its roots in the North Kildonan MB Church. To alleviate overcrowding 248 charter members built that church at 200 McIvor Avenue in 1976. In 1988 the membership was 383.[9] Thus the three MB churches in North Kildonan are related and all are getting to be large congregations, with each of them discussing plans for extension.

The General Conference Mennonites came in 1929, worshiped with the Mennonite Brethren for six years until 1935, and built their first church at 256 Devon Avenue. The original church, enlarged twice, still exists and is used as a private residence today. These early churches in North Kildonan were built during the Depression, so they are modest wooden buildings, quite unpretentious compared to newer churches today. Immigrants from both Europe and Paraguay caused considerable growth so the North Kildonan Mennonite congregation of 268 members built a basement for a new church into which they moved in 1956, their present location at 1131 Roch Street. Since then two additions have been made.[10]

Three other GC churches grew out of the North Kildonan Mennonite Church. In 1964 a group of 203 members, formerly from South America, left the North Kildonan Church to form Springfield Heights Mennonite Church, located at 570 Sharron Bay.[11] This largely German language congregation of Paraguayan immigrants created quite a different group. Another group within the Springfield Heights Church wanted more English for their children. They first met for worship in River East Collegiate in 1972, and by 1975 the congregation became autonomous with forty-three members. They completed their church building at 365 Edelweis in 1978, meeting as the Northdale Mennonite Fellowship.[12] By 1980 another group began to meet as the Douglas Mennonite Church located at 1517 Douglas, also a new daughter church of Springfield Heights and largely of Paraguayan immigrant origin. Another group has recently started meeting in the River East school conducting services in German.

The four MB and five GC churches in North Kildonan represent a considerable cluster of Mennonite churches near the original "Chicken and Dairy Village." Mennonites are more concentrated in this area residentially than any other part of greater Winnipeg. Out of these modest farming enterprises grew many businesses, which present another very interesting story to be discussed later in another chapter on business and economics. Indeed, an industrial park east of the Mennonite cluster is where a number of these Mennonite businesses are now located. However, North Kildonan has not spawned large numbers of other Mennonite educational, publication and conference institutions which is what happened in Elmwood, several miles farther south.

1928 -78 Cairn Commemorating the Settlement of the First Mennonite Settlement in North Kildonan on Edison (Photo: Leo Driedger)

5

ELMWOOD, THE MB
INSTITUTIONAL CENTER

The points of concentration in early Winnipeg Mennonite history represent residential and church clusters in the North End, West End and North Kildonan. It takes a while for concentrations of educational, media and conference institutions to develop. The first began to happen in Elmwood among the Mennonite Brethren some thirty years later in the latter 1940s.

Some of the Russian Mennonite immigrants of the 1920s, such as C.A. DeFehr, had done business in Russia and so began business in Winnipeg as well. In the course of his business DeFehr bought some land in Elmwood on the northeast side of the Red River near Point Douglas. He was extensively involved in most of the major Mennonite Brethren institutional beginnings, and provided sites of land for a cluster of institutions which developed on Talbot and Riverton Avenues across the Red River not far from downtown.

MB College and Collegiate

The Mennonite Brethren Bible College (MBBC) was established in Winnipeg in 1944. It was the first Mennonite higher educational institution on the college level in Canada. Numerous Bible schools and some high schools had already been established across Canada, especially in the 1930s, by various Mennonite groups to train young people in Bible knowledge on the elementary and high school levels. However, with the beginnings of urbanization, more youth continued their education and society became more complex, so there was an increased need to train leaders beyond high school.

In the United States the precedent was to establish these schools in towns, so beginning a Bible college in a large metropolis was a bold and unprecedented step in North America. Some of the Russian Mennonites who came to Canada in the 1920s had already entered universities and trade schools in Europe, so their education helped them compete in the larger city. The Mennonite Brethren actually debated whether the need for a higher education facility should be located in the small town of Winkler or the larger center of Winnipeg. The conference opted for Winnipeg where churches had been established and growing for thirty years.

The building on Talbot Avenue, purchased in 1944, is still being used. Since then the college facilities have expanded into a number of other buildings forming a campus on Riverton Avenue (see photo). While the curriculum included mostly biblical, theological, Christian education and music courses, some courses were also given in the Arts. By 1961 MBBC was affiliated with Waterloo Lutheran University in Ontario, and at present it is affiliated with the University of Winnipeg. The college draws students from across Canada and has an enrollment of 150 to 200 students, both full and part-time.[1]

In 1945 the Mennonite Brethren Collegiate Institute (MBCI) was established and the high school moved into its new building next door on Talbot Avenue in 1947.[2] While the school was established for MB students, other students also attend. The school offers the regular Manitoba high school curriculum, embellished with some religious and music offerings as well as chapel. These two schools, established in Elmwood for over forty years, were the first of a series of MB institutions which have since clustered in the area.

Christian Press and Periodicals

While Elmwood has become an educational center for Canadian Mennonite Brethren studies, it has also become the center for national MB publication and church periodicals. *Die Mennonitische Rundschau* came to Winnipeg in 1923 and was located in the West End at 672 Arlington for many years.[3] In 1940 the Rundschau Publishing House was reorganized into the Christian Press. In 1951 it relocated to Elmwood into a more spacious building at 159 Henderson Highway, a block away from the college and collegiate. *Die Rundschau* and the Christian Press had become part of the Mennonite Brethren conference and businessman C.A. DeFehr, longtime member of the board, was again able to provide land for the relocation.

The Christian Press became the Canadian MB publishing house and today several other periodicals are printed there. *The Mennonite Observer* was published from 1955-61, and in 1962 the conference began to publish *The Mennonite Brethren Herald*, which is still the official English paper of the Canadian MB conference.[4] The press prints two Mennonite periodicals, and the conference's Kindred Press publishes books and Christian literature for both Canadian and American audiences. The two periodicals are read across Canada and beyond.

MB Conference and Communications Offices.

With two schools, two papers and a press located in Elmwood, this Mennonite Brethren center continued to have a life of its own, attracting more institutions all the time. C.A. DeFehr again donated land so the North End congregation which worshiped on College Avenue could relocate next to the Christian Press in 1954. The Elmwood MB Church on 145 Henderson Highway has become a college church for many MBBC faculty and students.

In 1947 MBBC college students began the Gospel Light Hour, a radio broadcast which became affiliated with the Manitoba MB Conference. By 1966 the program was broadcast over nine stations in three provinces; at present there are English, Russian, German and Low German programs designed for a variety of audiences. English TV programming reaches a national audience.[6] Today this work is located in a new large MB Communications building at 225 Riverton Avenue, a block east of the college. The Manitoba MB Conference offices are located here as well, including staff of Manitoba missions and church extension.

The Canadian MB Conference offices are located at 169 Riverton on the second floor of one of the new college and conference buildings. The national church growth and evangelism, Christian education, and financial services of the conference are located in Winnipeg. Reorganization has placed more of the continental and world outreach and missions personnel at the Riverton address also. Thus Elmwood has become a major provincial, national and international MB conference headquarters.

6

COMING OF THE RURAL KANADIER

While a few of the first Mennonites who came in 1874 saw tiny Winnipeg, the descendants of these conservative Old Colony, Sommerfelder, Bergthaler, Kleine Gemeinde and Rudnerweider Mennonites from rural reserves came to the city only occasionally before World War II. Living in a city was considered taboo, the place where corruption and sin ran rampant. The *Kanadier* (the "Canadians," because they lived here for generations) as they were often called, were much slower in coming to urban centers than the Russian immigrants of the 1920s and 1950s. While the Russian Mennonites of the 1920s are very much a part of the two largest General Conference and Mennonite Brethren groups in Canada, many of the *Kanadier* of southern Manitoba who arrived earlier are heavily represented in the smaller conservative groups. Without the Russian Mennonites, there would likely be fewer than a dozen Mennonite churches in Winnipeg today. Let us trace the movements of some of these *Kanadier*.

Bethel Mennonite Mission

In January 1938 Benjamin Ewert made an announcement in three German Mennonite periodicals:

> . . . the undersigned (Benjamin Ewert) has conducted worship services in Winnipeg since the beginning of the year. These worship services are especially designed for

> Canadian-born Mennonites . . . . The undersigned plans to
> begin catechism instruction classes for Canadian-born youth
> in the beginning of March. It is hoped that Canadian-born
> youth be informed of this and encouraged to participate.[1]

Why this three-fold emphasis on Canadian-born Mennonites? This
was a special appeal to those who had come from rural Manitoba to
work and live in the city. As yet no Canadian-born Mennonite church
had been established in Winnipeg.

While the more conservative *Kanadier* in southern Manitoba were
reluctant to start churches in Winnipeg, some of their members were
beginning to move there. The depression of the 1930s forced many to
seek jobs in the city because unemployment in the rural areas was
severe. The Ewert brothers (Henry H. and Benjamin) who received
higher education in Kansas came to Manitoba in 1891 and 1892 respectively to teach and help guide the public education system. The brothers,
having more education, were soon asked by the church leaders to visit
university students and the renegade segment of the church who had
moved beyond the reserve to Winnipeg.[2] As early as 1907 some Mennonites from Winnipeg came back to the reserve to be baptized. By 1909
H.H. Ewert made a trip to the city to visit some of them, and sources sug-
gest that by 1915 some kind of group was beginning to form.[3] By 1920
he had served the group with a number of services.

In 1917 Benjamin Ewert was elected to the Missions Committee of
the Canadian General Conference, and by 1918 he spent some days
looking for students and other Mennonites in Winnipeg, where as many
as one hundred attended worship services. In 1921 he was hired to serve
as minister in Winnipeg, so he and his family moved there and held
monthly services. These Mennonites began to meet at the Reformed
Zion Church on Alexander Avenue. By 1923 Ewert was in touch with
112 Mennonite families, most of them of *Kanadier* origin. However, a
flood of Russian immigrants began attending these services, and before
long they swamped the group and the *Kanadier* no longer came.[4] "The
sociological factors that prevented easy amalgamation of Canadian-born
and Russian-born Mennonites were neither recognized nor understood.
The more aggressive and educated German-speaking Russian Mennonites overwhelmed the conservative migrants from southern
Manitoba to whom conversational German was a foreign language."[5]
Thus Ewert's first attempt at creating a *Kanadier* Mennonite church

began well, but it became part of the Schönwieser Mennonite church of the West End, now called the First Mennonite Church, made up of mostly Russian Mennonites.

In 1938 a second attempt was made at forming a *Kanadier* Mennonite church, which has resulted in the Bethel Mennonite Church. Benjamin Ewert again gathered twenty-one people together and they first met for worship in the Immanuel Baptist Church on Sargent and Sherbrook. Morning services were held in German and evening meetings in English. World War II brought many young Mennonite men into Winnipeg who did their conscientious objector service here. This greatly boosted attendance and activity at Bethel Mission, so that together with Isaac I. Friesen's arrival in 1943, the church began to grow considerably.[6]

In 1944 the Bethel Mission congregation bought their first building at the corner of Furby and Westminster. In 1956 they moved into a new structure on the corner of 870 Carter and Stafford where the church is still located. The first *Kanadier* Mennonite church was now firmly established in Winnipeg, considerably later than those churches begun by Russian Mennonite immigrants of the 1920s.

Newcomers from the East Reserve

Mennonites of the East Reserve, of which Steinbach is the major center today, were largely 1870s immigrants of *Die Kleine Gemeinde*, or Little Church. They began as a separate church in 1812 in Russia, and have since been renamed the Evangelical Mennonite Conference (EMC). Their main offices are in Steinbach, which today is known as the Automobile City, as business networks between Mennonites in Steinbach and Winnipeg have developed over the years. It is not surprising some EMCers would have moved to the big city.

There are four Evangelical Mennonite churches in Winnipeg, and services first began in 1951 in Wesley Chapel at the corner of Ellice and Beverly.[7] The group grew from six to one hundred in a year. In 1955 they purchased their first building at 741 Redwood Avenue, and their numbers grew so that by 1956 they purchased the Aberdeen Church in the North End where it is still located at 533 Aberdeen Avenue. While the Mennonite Brethren of Russian origin moved out of the North End in 1954, EMC *Kanadier* came to the area and are still located there.

The other three EMC churches are scattered throughout other parts of the city. Braeside EM Church is located at 1011 Munroe Avenue, an outgrowth of the Aberdeen Church.[8] In 1968 the first services were held in the new structure which is located in a fairly new suburb of East Kildonan. In 1963 the Crestview Fellowship Chapel began with a group meeting in the St. Charles School near the perimeter highway on the western outskirts of the city in St. James. In 1967 they built a new church at 271 Hamilton Avenue, which was extended in 1982. The fourth and most recent church began in 1976 when twenty-eight people met in the Agassiz Drive School in Fort Garry.[9] In 1977 they became an official group with twenty-six charter members and bought a small 7-Eleven convenience store where they worshiped for six years. In 1984 they built a new church on the same location, which is a block away from the University of Manitoba. Many young people attend the church and their college and career group is growing fast.

The Evangelical Mennonite Brethren (EMB) is an earlier branch from the *Kleine Gemeinde* in the Steinbach area and the second group to have moved to Winnipeg. They established two churches and have always stressed evangelism. The Christian Fellowship Chapel at 456 Osborne presently has a membership of about 131, while St. Vital Community Church was established almost thirty years ago and now has a membership of thirty-nine. Both churches do not include the name Mennonite, and recently the conference decided to make the designation optional. The now renamed EMB (Fellowship of Evangelical Bible Churches) conference is one of the smaller conferences and its churches in Winnipeg are also small.

Kanadier from the West Reserve

While the Evangelical Mennonites (EMC) represent the heart of the Mennonite East Reserve, the Old Colony Mennonites represent the major group to move into the western part of the West Reserve in the 1870s. However, the Old Colony Mennonites have not established a church in Winnipeg. They represent the most conservative of rural Mennonites, many of whom moved to Mexico in the 1920s. Those who remain still consider the city a dangerous place in which to live, and many live in southern Manitoba villages.

The Bergthaler who settled more in the eastern part of the West Reserve around Altona came to Winnipeg later, and many became members of the Bethel Mission Church. Of the 402 members in 1957, eighty (or twenty percent) were Bergthaler.[10] In 1957 several meetings were held and it was decided to start a Bergthaler church in Winnipeg. The group began meeting in the MB Edison church but a year later moved to Simcoe and St. Matthews in the West End area. This church became too small, so in 1960 they purchased a Pentecostal church at Sherbrook and Ross where they worshiped for twelve years. In 1973 they moved to their present location into a United Church building at 318 Home Street, when the name was changed to Home Street Mennonite Church.[11] They are presently members of the General Conference Mennonite Church. Because of severe crowding a new church was formed in 1967, named the Fort Garry Fellowship. This group met for many years at the Nazarene College and has since located in its new building at 150 Bayridge in Fort Richmond. These three churches include many Mennonites from the West Reserve, now amalgamated into the General Conference.

The Rudnerweider are a fifth group from the West Reserve who have moved to Winnipeg. In the 1930s change also came to the Sommerfelder and Old Colony Mennonites in rural southern Manitoba when four ministers experienced spiritual renewal and introduced changes in singing, style of sermons, services and dress.[12] Eventually they formed their new Rudnerweider church, which included 2,700 adults and children in 1937. Since then three Evangelical Mennonite Mission churches (EMMC), as they were renamed, have been established in Winnipeg. EMMCers first met with General Conference Mennonites, but in 1952 Rudnerweider ministers came to preach in the city once a month. In 1956 they began to meet separately and in 1957 established their own church at 232 Nassau Street where the enlarged Gospel Mennonite Church is still located. The Nassau church became too small, so by 1967 the Morrow Gospel Church was established at 51 Morrow, which in 1976 moved to its present location at 755 St. Anne's Road in a suburb of St. Vital.[13] The third EMMC church, Richmond Gospel Fellowship, was established in 1987 by a few families from these two parent congregations. This group meets at the Fort Richmond Collegiate.

The EMMC Canadian Conference offices were originally established in Altona in 1964. They then relocated in Winnipeg at 292 Victor Street, then in 1971 to 859 Sargent Avenue (which is now the MCC Thrift Shop), and finally to 526 Macmillan Avenue, next door to the original Nassau Gospel Mennonite Church.[14] At present three Mennonite denominations have located their national head offices in Winnipeg, including the Mennonite Brethren in Elmwood, the General Conference Mennonites in Tuxedo, and the Evangelical Mennonite Mission Conference in Crescentwood.

While the Old Colony Mennonites of the West Reserve have not yet established a church in Winnipeg, the Sommerfelder have begun two churches, the first at 345 Simcoe Street and a second in East Kildonan. Enough members of these conservative Mennonites have moved to Winnipeg in the 1980s so large numbers are attending even though it took them longer to make that move.

7

THE SUBURBAN DIASPORA

Gibson Winter, in *The Suburban Captivity of the Churches*,[1] argues that over time Protestants especially tend to become more educated, better off financially and move to better residential areas. Therefore, as members can afford better housing, they move to the suburbs and take their churches with them. Catholics and Anglicans who are committed to parishes in every part of the city tend not to follow this pattern. Winter suggests this movement to the suburbs is unfortunate because the inner city needs people who can help.[2] If Winter is correct, and since Mennonites are very congregationally oriented, we would expect Mennonites to move toward the suburbs also. Let us examine some of the evidence.

Circulation of the North End Saints.

Seventy years ago Mennonites began their first churches in the North End, today considered to be one of the older and more central parts of Winnipeg. The first location was on Burrows, four blocks from Selkirk, a major business section of the North End and only eight blocks from the CPR railroad. They next moved to College Avenue, four blocks north into somewhat newer housing in the 1930s, where they built a much larger church. During the 1950s they moved out of the North End "Foreign Quarter" into Elmwood, not farther from the center of the city but closer to the river near Point Douglas, the first most prestigious part of residential Winnipeg where the church is still located. This abandonment of the North End would clearly support Winter's thesis. The North End MB Mission now has become the college church of the Mennonite Brethren.

Interestingly, while the earlier Mennonites moved out of the North End in the fifties, the *Kanadier* who came to the city much later moved back into the area in the 1950s. The Burrows Bethel Church has also moved into the area recently, using a large older brick United Church building with spacious architecture, considerably more prestigious looking than their former smaller wooden structure. This seems to represent a new wrinkle in upward mobility with their pipe organ. The recent Chinese immigrants, who have formed the Winnipeg Chinese MB Church, worship in a small, older residence near the river in the North End as well. If and when members of these three churches become more upwardly mobile, will they also move toward the suburbs into larger newer facilities? Time will tell. There is considerable evidence that Winter's thesis is operating among Mennonites in the North End.

CMBC Invasion of the Anglo South

Before World War II, Mennonites located in the multicultural areas of the North End, West End and North Kildonan, north of the central city. After the second great war, they began to invade southern and western parts of Winnipeg which were strongholds of the Anglo-Saxons. The higher status areas of contemporary Winnipeg are located in the southern parts like Tuxedo and River Heights. A hundred years ago Point Douglas was the high status residential area, followed by the West End.[3] However, when the CPR railroad came into Winnipeg in the 1880s, these residential areas became less desirable and new status areas developed south across the Assiniboine River into River Heights, and finally south and west to Tuxedo. Before the 1950s no Mennonite churches were located south of the Assiniboine.

When the Canadian Mennonite Bible College (CMBC) began in 1947, classes commenced in the Bethel Mission Church on Furby Street at the doorstep of Montgomery Point. Fifty years earlier before the dominance of the automobile, this was one of Winnipeg's high status residential areas. Two years later, the college moved just across the river to 515 Wellington Crescent into a three-storey mansion which was in Winnipeg's most prestigious older residential area. This was the first entrance next to the river into southern Anglo-Saxon territory. In 1956 CBMC moved even deeper into Anglo-Saxon territory where it is now located at 600 Shaftesbury in Tuxedo.[4]

This CMBC location is not yet as large a center of Canadian GC institutions as the Elmwood MB center, but it is moving in that direction. The offices of the national Conference of Mennonites in Canada located at the campus in 1961; the Conference of Mennonites of Manitoba offices are in the process of moving there from 1483 Pembina Highway. The Mennonite Faith and Life radio communications will be transferred with the Manitoba offices. The Mennonite Heritage Center, which houses the Conference of Mennonites archives, was built on the Tuxedo campus in 1978.[5]

The editorial offices of several General Conference Mennonite newspapers are also located at CMBC. *Der Bote*, the German paper of the GCs, moved its editorial offices from Saskatchewan to Tuxedo in 1977 where it is still edited.[6] The editorial office of the English periodical *The Mennonite* was located on the campus between 1971 and 1986 when it moved back to Kansas.

Suburban Captivity of Mennonite Churches

While one of the two Mennonite colleges has moved into the suburbs of Tuxedo, after World War II roughly one-fourth of the forty-seven Mennonite churches have followed into newer areas on the outer suburban rim of the greater metropolitan area. Whether the move of CMBC to Tuxedo was merely an opportunity to find cheaper land or whether it reflected upward mobility of Mennonites in general may be difficult to discern. However, the movement of a dozen Mennonite churches to the suburbs, where they are building new larger structures, seems to be clear evidence of upwardly mobile better-to-do members. Winter's thesis that Protestants with their congregational polity tend to take their churches with them as they become better off and move to the newer more affluent areas seems clearly evident among Winnipeg Mennonites.

A number of the newer North Kildonan churches are moving north into larger buildings, including McIvor MB, Douglas Avenue Mennonite and River East MB. Two other MB congregations on the east side include Valley Gardens Community Church and Transcona Community Church. Portage Avenue MB, Westwood Community Church (MB) and Crestview Fellowship (EMC) would be examples in the west and St. James areas, while Charleswood Mennonite is an example in Charleswood south of the Assiniboine.[7] Sterling Mennonite Fellowship, Morrow Gospel (EMMC) and St. Vital Community EMB are examples in St. Vital.

The best example of the suburban Mennonite trend can be found in Fort Garry, the heart of Anglo-Saxon Winnipeg. Fort Garry MB, Fort Garry Fellowship, Fort Garry EMC and Richmond Gospel Fellowship (EMMC) represent four different Mennonite groups located in this suburb. While the social status of Fort Garry is not as high as Tuxedo, it does include the University of Manitoba. At least two of these churches have had some success in drawing students, which calls for dynamic leadership and more creative worship activities. Fort Garry MB is located on the west side of the university and Fort Garry EMC on the southeast side, easily accessible from the campus. Both draw some university faculty, which is also the case with Fort Garry Fellowship. All three have now moved to larger worship and educational facilities.

The Fort Garry MB Church is the best example of Mennonites moving from the central core of the city to the suburbs. The church originated as the Gospel Light MB Church located in the heart of Winnipeg on Logan and Ellen, also referred to as Logan Mission. It began as a Sunday school staffed by students from MBBC, and worship services were first held in 1953.[8] In 1959 the twenty-six charter members bought a church on the corner of McMillan and Arbuthnot in Fort Rouge, just south of the Assiniboine River. This represented a considerable shift away from the central area into the higher status Anglo-Saxon south of moderately old residential housing. In the meantime, others joined from Southend MB and elsewhere, so the membership grew substantially from fifty-seven to 165 in eighteen months. In 1963 the church moved farther south into a new building in the suburb of Fort Garry near the university, where it is still located at 1771 Pembina Highway. This is perhaps the most dramatic example to demonstrate Winter's suburban captivity thesis.

8

BUSINESS AND WORK

Some claim there are more than 1,000 Mennonite businesses in Winnipeg, the majority being in the building trades.[1] Mennonites have entered practically all forms of business, but we can only touch on some of the larger prominent ones in home furnishings, wood and furniture manufacturing, metal products, transportation, building and realty.

Furniture and Appliances

C.A. DeFehr was a successful businessman in farm machinery in Russia. When he came to Winnipeg in 1926 he established a business at 159 Princess Street in downtown Winnipeg.[2] He began by selling imported German separators and hardware, which soon expanded so he had to move to larger quarters at 124-6 Princess and later 86 Princess Street. His three sons, (A.C., C.C., W.C.) and one son-in-law (B.B. Fast) all joined the business so until 1963 it included five partners working together under C.A. DeFehr and Sons. Soon they expanded into appliances, farm and household supplies, furniture and heating equipment.[3] Grandsons later joined the business and it expanded to Brandon, Manitoba; Saskatoon and Regina, Saskatchewan; Edmonton, Alberta; and Fargo, North Dakota. In 1963 the four sons and shareholders became separate corporations under the umbrella of DeFehr Furniture and Appliances at 86 Princess, where the head offices are today. The business is now headed by Arthur DeFehr and Neil Fast, grandsons of C.A.

(All photos by Leo Driedger)

Mennonite

CHURCHES
IN NORTH WINNIPEG

Burrows Mennonite Brethren
River East Mennonite Brethren
McIvor Mennonite Brethren

North Kildonan Mennonite Brethren
Aberdeen Evangelical Mennonite
Elmwood Mennonite Brethren

(All photos by Leo Driedger)

Mennonite
CHURCHES
IN CENTRAL WINNIPEG

Christian Fellowship
Home Street Mennonite
Erin Street Mission Chapel

Portage Avenue Mennonite Brethren
First Mennonite
Sargent Avenue Mennonite

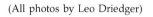
(All photos by Leo Driedger)

Mennonite
CHURCHES
IN SOUTH WINNIPEG

Fort Garry Mennonite Fellowship
Fort Garry Mennonite Brethren
Winnipeg Chinese Mennonite

Richmond Gospel Fellowship
Bethel Mennonite
Fort Garry Evangelical Mennonite

Some Mennonite

BUSINESSES
IN WINNIPEG

Fellowship Bookcenter
d'8 Schtove Restaurant
All-Fab Building Components plant

A.A. DeFehr at the Chicken Barn (Palliser)
Palliser Furniture
Palliser Furniture Worker
(All photos by Leo Driedger except All-Fab photo and

(All photos by Leo Driedger)

Mennonite
HOSPITALS & HOMES

Donwood South MB Apartments
Bethania Mennonite Personal Care Home
Arlington House

Donwood Manor Personal Care Home
Bethel Place Apartments
Concordia Hospital

Mennonite
SCHOOLS

Mennonite Chair and Menno Simons Center
Mennonite Elementary School
Mennonite Brethren Collegiate

Canadian Mennonite Bible College
Mennonite Brethren Bible College
Westgate Mennonite Collegiate
(All photos by Leo Driedger)

Mennonite
OFFICES & CENTERS

Mennonite Brethren Communications
Evangelical Mennonite Mission Conference
Mennonite Heritage Center and Archives
(All photos by Leo Driedger except Heritage

The Christian Press
Conference of Mennonites in Manitoba
Mennonite Brethren Conference,
   College and Archives

(All photos by Leo Driedger)

Mennonite
SERVICES & OUTREACH

Mennonite Mediation Services and
Mennonite Reporter
Mary-Martha Girls Home (last one)

MCC Community Self-Help Thrift Shop
on Sargent
Mennonites at the Winnipeg Peace March
Mennonite Central Committee Canada

DeFehr. In 1989 DeFehr's employed 140 workers (seventy in Winnipeg).[4]

C.A. DeFehr was also extensively involved in the education and mission of the church. He had an important hand in developing the Mennonite Brethren institutional center in Elmwood. In 1954 the Elmwood MB Church moved to DeFehr property, close to the Christian Press, the MBBC and MBCI. For many years he was a deacon in the Elmwood MB Church, a member on the MB City Mission board, Maria-Martha Home, MB conference, Christian Press, MBBC board, and Mennonite Central Committee, which he and his wife served with for a number of years.

While DeFehr Furniture and Appliances is in retailing, Palliser is in furniture manufacturing. Palliser began in North Kildonan when Abram A. DeFehr, a nephew of C.A. DeFehr, sold his car and bought woodworking equipment and set up shop in a chicken barn at 234 Kingsway in 1944.[6] In 1948 he moved A.A. DeFehr Manufacturing to 400 Edison Avenue where the business expanded (now it's a shopping center). By 1963 this became too small so it was relocated to the industrial park east of the Mennonite community with head offices located at 55 Vulcan Avenue. It has been renamed Palliser Furniture Ltd.[7]

Palliser Furniture dominates the North Kildonan industrial park and is Canada's largest manufacturer of wood household furniture in the West. A.A. DeFehr is chairman of the board and his three sons Frank, Art (president) and David have all joined Palliser. The business employs 1,300 workers and gross revenues have increased from $54 million in 1984 to over $100 million in 1987.[8] Palliser products are marketed in all ten Canadian provinces through some 1,300 retail outlets with plants in Winnipeg, Calgary, AB and Fargo, ND in the US.

Art DeFehr was involved in MCC development work in Nepal, Thailand and Ethiopia, and David DeFehr served under MCC in Nigeria. Art has also served in a United Nations diplomatic post for refugees in Somalia, became the founding chair of the Winnipeg Canadian Foodgrains Bank in 1976, and is currently president of Economic Development International. Palliser has a profit-sharing arrangement which paid their workers over $2 million dollars in 1986 and a stock ownership plan for senior employees. It also employs many handicapped persons.[9]

Metal Works and Products

While the DeFehrs were developing appliance and furniture businesses downtown and in North Kildonan, J.J. Klassen, a former teacher in Russia, was the first to begin business in the West End by peddling wares and starting metal works in a basement on the corner of Home and Notre Dame.[10] He soon moved to 889 Erin where Monarch Industries Ltd. is now located. His two sons, John (joined in 1942) and Ernest (1949) are presently president and chairman of the business, and two of their sons, Richard and Gregory, are also with Monarch.[11] Monarch employs 350 workers, 200 in Winnipeg and 150 in two factories in Winkler. Monarch is in casting and fabricating motor and concrete mixers selling in twenty-five countries of the world. John Klassen was president of the Manitoba Centennial Committee and presently chairs the First Mennonite congregation.

Klassen Manufacturing Ltd. began a year later in 1936 in North Kildonan, originally located at 421 Edison as part of the Mennonite settlements. It has since moved to the industrial park at 60 Burnett where it employs fifteen people engaged in metal stamping with sales to Palliser and western Canadian companies.[12] Both of these metal businesses were started in the 1930s during the Depression.

Transportation

After World War II Mennonite business in Winnipeg started to mushroom. A.J. Thiessen began buying chickens, eggs and hides in 1932 in southern Manitoba, transporting them to the city. He also started Wawanesa Mutual Insurance and a general store.[13] By 1946 Thiessen received a bus franchise operating between the West Reserve and Winnipeg where he and his brothers John and Peter located the head office. In 1964 they began Flyer Industries, a bus factory, since taken over by the Manitoba government. In 1965 they established Circle Tours which in 1989 offered twenty-five package tours. By 1969 A.J. Thiessen Transportation was renamed Grey Goose Bus Lines Ltd., running up to seventy buses in the province. In 1971 they went public, merging with Laidlaw Transportation in 1973. Thiessen's sons Ronald and Bernard (now president) joined the business in 1954 and 1966 respectively.[14]

Grey Goose has since branched out into many other areas, including Yellow Cab in Edmonton and Calgary with more than 800 cabs. In 1971 the Thiessens purchased Acme Sanitation Services in Winnipeg which is now managed by son William Thiessen; in 1978 they purchased Byers Trucking Lines in Alberta with 250 units; in 1988 they began operating Grey Lines Tours on Vancouver Island; and in 1989 they began boat cruise services. Grey Goose and its affiliates employ 4000 employees (300 in Winnipeg) running 2,800 units between Ontario and British Columbia, with revenues of approximately $125 million annually.

A.J. Thiessen has served Mennonites extensively on the Mennonite Collegiate Institute board in Gretna; he led in the formation of radio station CFAM; served many years on school boards and chambers of commerce; and ran for government office in provincial and federal elections, serving on numerous governmental committees.[15] All five of Thiessen's children and grandsons Paul, Andrew and Lyndon have been involved in the business. Bernie has also served in Mennonite missions, youth, camp and Mennonite school boards. William and Carolyn have been heavily involved in music.[16]

While A.J. Thiessen began trucking and bus services out of Altona in the West Reserve, Don Reimer, grandson of storekeeper P.B. Reimer of Steinbach and the East Reserve started trucking services between Winnipeg and Windsor in 1952. The company has grown to be Reimer Express Enterprises Ltd. with head offices located at 1400 Inkster in Winnipeg.[17] The company employs approximately 2,600 people of whom 700 are located in Winnipeg. Delbert and Gerald later joined their brother Don, all three are sons of Frank F. Reimer. Four of their sons - Jim, Ross, Doug and Darcy - are also involved with the company. Don continues as president and chief executive officer.[18]

Reimer Express Enterprises Ltd. is comprised of nine companies, including the "flagship" operation Reimer Express Lines which serves all provinces from Quebec to British Columbia as well as the US. In addition the group of companies includes Inter-City Truck Lines (Canada) Inc., Trans Canada Truck Lines Inc., Canadian Great Western Express Inc., Fleet Express Services, Fast As Flite, Big Freight and Fast-Pac.[19]

Kildonan Wood Products and Crafts

Since the first Mennonite community of chicken and truck farmers began in North Kildonan in 1928, many Mennonites have started businesses in the area of wood products, Palliser Furniture being a prime example. Numerous other wood product businesses have emerged. Cornelius Huebert started selling feed, hay, flour, coal and houses between Devon and Oakland in those early days, but later went into lumber sales and built the first fibre-board manufacturing plant in western Canada.[20] John Dyck began building wooden boxes for fish packing which became Dyck's Containers and Forest Products Limited. Three other Dyck brothers also went into business in North Kildonan: Isaac with Hawthorne Woodworks, Jacob in garden tools and Abram dealing with chains.[21]

In 1936 Henry Redekopp started a flour and feed store. It expanded to groceries in 1937 and in 1951 into Redekopp Lumber, a wood and lumber retail outlet on the west side of Henderson Highway. The building was demolished and the area turned into a large shopping center.[22] Allmar and Willmar are two firms which are branches of these original Redekopp enterprises. Allmar Distributors Limited was born in 1954 as a lumber wholesale distributor. It is now run by Redekopp's two sons Ed and Art at 287 Riverton Avenue, while the other four Redekopp family children are shareholders. Allmar is now involved in supplying building materials and architectural hardware.[23] It has 120 employees in Winnipeg (seventy-five percent), Regina, Saskatoon, Edmonton, Calgary and Vancouver (twenty percent being Mennonite).

A second branch of Redekopp Lumber continues as Willmar Window Industries with Bill Fast, Redekopp's son-in-law, as president. Fast is also a grandson of C.A. DeFehr. Fast worked in the Redekopp distributing business for ten years when he decided in 1963 it was time to get into manufacturing windows.[24] Willmar (the name is derived from William and Margaret) Windows Industries is located at 485 Watt in East Kildonan with 400 employees (225 in Winnipeg), with branches in Regina, Saskatoon, Calgary and Edmonton. Bill Fast is a member of numerous Mennonite school boards, provincial and Canadian boards of trustees, and his local church council.[25]

Kitchen Craft was founded in 1971 by Herb Buller and John

Rademaker and is located at 1180 Springfield Road in North Kildonan. It is a more recent first generation manufacturing and distribution company of kitchen cabinetry with major emphasis on modular and custom cabinetry.[26] They employ 325 workers in their Winnipeg plant and store with branches in Brampton, Regina, Saskatoon, Edmonton, Calgary, Vancouver, Fresno, Minneapolis and the Dakotas.[27] This is one of the few Mennonite businesses which has not started as a family network.

All-Fab Building Components located at 1755 Dugald Road and Woodland Supply and Manufacturing at 867 McLeod represent somewhat smaller businesses working in wood products. All-Fab is a company of five Mennonite partners which began in 1970, employing 110 workers with total annual sales of $14 million in 1988. All-Fab manufactures roof trusses, while Olympic Building Systems is their sales arm with revenue of $14 million in 1988.[28] Woodland Supply began as Bock and Regehr Construction and became Woodland Supply in 1965, employing eighty-five workers with sales of $10 million in 1988.[29] One Bock and two Regehr sons have joined the business recently. Their production includes milling mouldings and trimmings for staircases and kitchen cabinet casings. They have sales branches in Thunder Bay and Vancouver.

Building and Realty

Albert DeFehr, past president of the Manitoba and Canadian Home Builders associations, estimates there are at least 1,000 Mennonites involved in home building.[30] We examined the membership list of the Manitoba association and found many Mennonite names. While Mennonites entered the distribution and manufacture of furniture and wood products earlier, home building became popular in the 1950s when Mennonites with construction skills and requiring minimal capital started in the home building business after arriving in Winnipeg.

Martin and Miriam Bergen came to Canada in 1953 and started running a painting business. In 1958 it became Viceroy Decorating Limited under Miriam, located at 1110 Henderson Highway. Martin soon began Marlborough Development Corporation Limited in 1962 with head offices located at the same address. They both concentrated on building apartment blocks and constructed thirty-five buildings with

7,000 suites by 1989.[31] In 1963 they started Edison Rental Agency to serve many of these apartments. They also built and operate Royal Crown (Revolving) Restaurant located at 83 Garry, Tiffani's Restaurant at 133 Niakwa and Martini's Restaurant at 319 Sargent. They employ 160 workers: one hundred in the rental business, fifty-five in the decorating business, and five in building working mainly with sub-contractors.[32]

Qualico Homes, one of the larger companies, was well underway by the early 1960s operating as Quality Construction with David Friesen as president. Its head offices are located at 30 Speers in St. Boniface. Friesen has recently been active in establishing the Winnipeg Mennonite Elementary School, the Chair of Mennonite Studies at the University of Winnipeg, and Menno Simons College.

In 1981 William C. DeFehr sold out of the C.A. DeFehr business and went into real estate with his son Albert. Albert DeFehr began Red River Realty in 1970 and the four home building companies of Belleville Homes (1972), Manor Homes (1983), Castle Homes (1984) and Wellington Homes (1987) with 150 employees located in Winnipeg, Calgary, Edmonton and Vancouver.[33] Albert was active on the MCC Canada board for eleven years (seven years as treasurer), continuing the interests of his grandfather C.A. DeFehr.

There are numerous other businesses which could be mentioned. Jim Penner has four grocery stores, one located in North Kildonan employing 125 workers at Penner Foods. They have just completed an office building and warehouse in Transcona.[34] There are a number of restaurants such as d'8 Schtove on Pembina Highway which specialize in Mennonite foods, and Julia DeFehr recently opened Cafe Beignet catering to the after-concert trade. Kona Enterprises Limited is involved in the acquisition and development of real estate investment and was founded by David Epp and his sons. There are a number of Mennonite travel agencies including Menno Travel, Assiniboine Travel, Bonaventure Travel, Klassen Travel and Reidy Travel Services.

The dozen largest Mennonite businesses in Winnipeg which we have just introduced employ over 10,000 workers. A more intensive study of the more than 1,000 other Mennonite businesses needs to be researched. What is clear is that about seventy-five percent of the Mennonite businesses are family networks with fathers, sons, and in some cases daughters and grandchildren extensively involved. Interestingly, the individualism required for creative business has been well balanced by corporate family networks which require cooperation and teamwork. Many Mennonites in business are also heavily involved in the support of the church and its institutions. Their financial and leadership support is clearly evident, not to mention the jobs they provide for many people in the community.

One of the many construction companies owned by Mennonites during the construction of the addition to MBCI (Photo: MB Herald)

9

HOSPITALS AND HOMES

Mennonites who arrived in the latter 1920s had been engaged in considerable development of institutions including hospitals and homes for the elderly and disabled. Being used to having their own institutions, they were quick to provide hospital care. Personal care homes developed somewhat later in Winnipeg.

Concordia Hospital

A group of Mennonites rented a house at 291 Machray Avenue to start a five bed maternity hospital as early as 1928. Less than a dozen years after the first Mennonite church was organized (1917) and at the very beginning of Mennonite settlement in the West End (1926) and North Kildonan (1928), Mennonites already had started their first medical institution which is known today as Concordia Hospital. By 1930, two years later, a larger house was purchased at 720 Beverley Street with nine beds plus facilities for minor surgery.[1] Six years after the founding, the society purchased the former Winnipeg Sanatorium at 400 Desalaberry Street with a fifty bed capacity. In 1953 twenty-three more beds were added.

In 1974 they moved into a newly constructed 134 bed hospital located at 1095 Concordia Avenue in North Kildonan. In 1987 550 people were employed there, with 3,917 admissions for that year, 3,868 surgical procedures and 1,117 home care visits made.[2] The hospital includes departments in anesthesia, dentistry, family practice, medicine, pediatrics, radiology and surgery. Obstetrics, the original purpose of the hospital, has been closed due to governmental rearrangements. In 1988 the hospital was in a major expansion program to build sixty more beds. The hospital is run by a board of sixteen members. Approximately one-third of the patients are Mennonites. About eighty-five doctors have admitting privileges, a dozen of them being Mennonite. Concordia is an integral part of the nine member hospital council in Winnipeg.

Bethania Homes in East Kildonan

Many of the early farm and immigrant Mennonites tended to keep their elderly parents with them in their homes during the first generation. However, by 1945, 400 of these same immigrants who started Concordia Hospital also joined together to begin the Bethania Nursing Home located five miles north of Middlechurch on the west bank of the Red River. By 1970 Bethania was relocated to 1045 Concordia Avenue, just adjacent to Concordia Hospital. The Bethania Mennonite Personal Care Home, Inc. started with sixty-eight beds, which expanded to one hundred beds in 1970 and 150 beds in 1987.[3]

About two-thirds of the 150 residents in Bethania are of German background; almost half are Mennonite. The purpose of the home is to provide those who can no longer live alone in their own homes, a place to stay, nursing, counselling, pastoral care and care for those who are mentally handicapped. A twelve member board selected from the Mennonite Benevolent Society directs the operations including auxiliary, dental, food, housekeeping, laundry services, medical, maintenance, pharmacy and nursing services, social work and pastoral care. In 1989 they opened a six-story building with suites providing independent living. The fifty-three suite Bethania House includes one and two bedroom suites for those who need little care. Located between the hospital and the home, they have access to medical and social services.

Mennonite Houses in the West End

Three Mennonite houses for the elderly cluster around First Mennonite Church in the West End. Sunset House, established in 1968, is directly attached to First Mennonite Church by a corridor and is operated by the church. There are thirty-seven units including thirty-two bachelor and five one-bedroom apartments at a very modest flat rate price. Since First Mennonite is a large 1,400 member church, there are a number of pastors who are nearby for counselling. About fifty percent of the occupants are Mennonite, the average age is eighty years, and seventy-five percent are women.[4]

Arlington House located at 880 Arlington was established in 1973. The same board operates both Sunset and Arlington houses. Arlington House is adjacent to Sunset with 121 units including one hundred bachelor and twenty one-bedroom apartments. About sixty percent of the residents are German-speaking; about fifty percent are Mennonite. Rental rates in Arlington are higher than in Sunset, but still quite reasonable.

The third home for the elderly, Autumn House, is located at 790 Wellington. It was established in 1979 by the Mennonite Benevolent Society which runs the Bethania homes. It is a residence more like Donwood South for persons with higher incomes. There are sixty-eight units: eleven bachelor, forty-seven one bedroom and ten two bedroom apartments. About seventy-five percent of the residents are German-speaking with approximately sixty-five percent being Mennonite.[5]

All three houses have tenant coordinators. Meals are provided three times a week, made possible by eighty volunteers from both inside and outside the houses. There is a tenant association which helps plan Bible studies, weekly bingos, and organizes physical exercises and games such as shuffleboard, carpet bowling and other activities.[6]

Mennonite Brethren Geriatric Association

More recently there has been an explosion of Mennonite care homes, and the Mennonite Brethren Geriatric Association is a good example. The twelve MB churches of Winnipeg developed four such facilities in less than twenty years. In 1970 they opened an eighty-one bed personal care home named Donwood Manor in North Kildonan at 171 Donwood Drive. This home provides three and four levels of care which calls for continuing medical attention supervised by a professional nursing staff. A majority of the residents require help with ambulation and feeding.[7]

A smaller number of persons who require level 2 care where long term care is needed but the needs are less severe. Donwood Manor has 112 staff working both full-time and part-time. Over half of the residents are Mennonite, the average age in 1988 was eighty-five years, and females outnumbered males six to one. A variety of services are provided.

In 1974 150 apartments of enriched elderly persons' housing was constructed adjoining the Personal Care Home located at 165 Donwood Avenue. Here residents live in their own one or two bedroom apartments fairly self-sufficiently but within easy access of eating, medical and social care facilities. In 1988 the average age was eighty years, about forty percent were Mennonite, and women outnumbered men two to one.[8]

Donwood South, a third facility, includes 104 apartments at 1245 Henderson Highway. These apartments for seniors provide more opportunity for independence. The average age in 1988 was seventy-five years and more than half of the occupants were of Mennonite background. These one and two bedroom apartments are somewhat more expensive and are designed for those who are better off and need less care.

In 1988 the Mennonite Brethren Geriatric Association opened Donwood West located at 1460 Portage Avenue. This was the first project in Manitoba where seniors could purchase one or two bedroom apartments. There are sixty units available under a life lease program.[9] Of the four Donwoods, this is the only one located outside of North Kildonan.

Bethel Place in South Winnipeg

Bethel Place is the first Mennonite facility for the elderly located south of the Assiniboine River and also the first developed mainly by Kanadier Mennonites. It is located at 445 Stafford Street and was built in 1980. It is an apartment block designed for retirement living with 140 apartments (mostly one bedroom). A total of 166 residents lived there in 1988, thirty men and 136 women. The place is run by a staff of eleven, six of them full-time, plus seventy volunteers.[10] Bethel Place includes a dining facility, day care nursery and crafts store plus numerous other pastoral, social and recreational activities and services.

Most of the ten Winnipeg Mennonite homes and places of care

were built with grants from the provincial government. However, these homes are expected to operate largely on the financial payments of residents and some donations from the Mennonite churches. Mennonites usually provide the majority of the staff and volunteer services. Government grants stipulate these facilities must be open to all applicants, but the philosophy and control of these institutions is largely directed by Mennonites who build, design, organize, maintain and operate them.

10

EDUCATION AND SCHOOLS

Two collegiates were established early in the small towns of Gretna,
Manitoba and Rosthern, Saskatchewan, similar to the early colleges established in the US. At the time, starting Mennonite high schools and
American colleges in towns when churches were often placed in the
open prairies was an important step away from the farm. Numerous
Bible schools were started later in small towns, especially in the 1930s
when the Russian Mennonites had limited funds in the Depression but
found the need for religious instruction at the elementary and high
school levels. Almost no one went to college or university at that time.
However, after World War II, with some Mennonites entering the city,
instruction on a higher level was required.

Mennonite Bible Colleges

Two colleges were established in Winnipeg, one by the Mennonite
Brethren in 1944 and the other by the Conference of Mennonites in
1947, an unprecedented development in a larger city in North America.
Since nearby Winkler in Manitoba was the first Canadian Mennonite
Brethren settlement, it seemed natural to start a college in Winnipeg.
The Winkler Mennonites had already begun mission work in 1913, and
in 1944 five Mennonite churches, including two Mennonite Brethren,
already existed in Winnipeg. A.H. Unruh, the respected Bible teacher at
Winkler Bible School, became the first Mennonite Brethren Bible Col-

lege president.[1]

Three years later in 1947, the Conference of Mennonites established the Canadian Mennonite Bible College. For many reasons, including Manitoba's larger Mennonite rural hinterland and the regional location closer to Ontario, Winnipeg again was chosen. Both colleges were established mostly by Russian Mennonites who saw the need for college education and were more heavily concentrated on the prairies. The establishment of these two colleges in the city gave urban Mennonites an enormous boost. J.A. Toews summarized the influence of MBBC in Canada:

> The spiritual impact of the Mennonite Brethren Bible College on the growth and development of the Mennonite Brethren Church can be seen, at least in part from the following statistics . . . in missionary service 106; in the preaching ministry 102; in the teaching ministry 241; in ministry of music 51. In addition hundreds of former students are active in church and Sunday school work. Practically all missionaries who have been commissioned by Canadian Mennonite Brethren churches for service in foreign fields during the last 25 years have received a part or all of their training in the Bible College.[2]

While I have not found similar statistics for CMBC, the report would most likely be very similar. The influence of these two colleges on Canadian Mennonite leadership is profound indeed.

The two colleges are engaged in several interesting cooperative programs. In 1988 six faculty, three from CMBC and three from MBBC, taught courses in which students from both colleges enrolled and attended. The two colleges are also involved in a Service Education program sponsored by MCC Canada along with Conrad Grebel College in Ontario and Columbia Bible College in British Columbia. Here certificates can be earned in preparation for overseas service.

In the 1988-89 school year there were 155 full-time and thirty-eight part-time students attending CMBC and ninety-five full-time and 125 part-time students studying at MBBC, for a total of 413 students.[3]

Relating to the Universities

Two of the three universities in the Province of Manitoba are located in Winnipeg. The University of Manitoba is the major university located in

Fort Garry with a full-time student body of 15,000 and 8,200 part-time students for a total of 23,100. The University of Winnipeg, formerly United College, is located downtown at 515 Portage Avenue with 2,700 full-time and 6,800 part-time students in 1988-89. A count of 1,420 Mennonite student names were found attending the University of Manitoba in 1988; Mennonite student names at the University of Winnipeg were not available but there are many there as well.[4] A majority of these Mennonite students at the two universities come from Winnipeg. There are 113 faculty with Mennonite names at the University of Manitoba and eighteen at the University of Winnipeg. Many of these are active Mennonites.[5]

The two Mennonite colleges in the city are affiliated with the two universities. CMBC is a teaching center of the University of Manitoba and MBBC is affiliated with the University of Winnipeg. MBBC is a cooperating institution and CMBC is a partner in a Seminary Consortium with Nazarene College and the University of Winnipeg, where students may study at the graduate level towards a Master's degree in religion.

University Mennonite Chair and Studies Center

In 1977 the Chair of Mennonite Studies was established at the University of Winnipeg, supported by the David Friesen Foundation and the Multicultural Directorate of the federal government; each contributed to an endowment of $600,000. Harry Loewen, the first and present professor in that Chair, and an advisory committee have developed courses on Mennonites involving annual guest lectureships, research and publications on Mennonites, and have begun the *Journal of Mennonite Studies* which appears annually. This Chair, which has been in existence for a dozen years, has helped the scholarly community to focus on Mennonite research and has created awareness of such studies among students.

In 1985 a Mennonite Studies Center was started at the University of Winnipeg as well, located at 380 Spence Street. At present it includes three staff persons focusing on an extension of Mennonite research, the endowment of Distinguished Visiting Professors, and plans to develop courses in conflict resolution and social and economic development studies.[6] The center is the beginning of a project for establishing Menno

63

Simons College in 1989. A charter has already been secured and there are plans for four more staff appointments.

Mennonite Collegiates

A year after MBBC was founded, a private high school was begun in 1945 as the Mennonite Brethren Collegiate Institute. At first the classes were held in the college, but by 1947 the collegiate moved into its own premises next door at 173 Talbot, being part of the beginnings of the MB institutional cluster in Elmwood.[7] The high school teaches the Manitoba curriculum with the addition of chapel, choral, history and Bible courses. In the 1988-89 school year twenty-eight teachers taught 461 students, most of them of Mennonite background. Students have competed well in debating and regional athletics beyond the MBCI walls.

Westgate Mennonite Collegiate, the second Mennonite high school in the city, is located at 86 Westgate. It is operated by eleven Mennonite churches of Winnipeg belonging to the Conference of Mennonites of Manitoba. The school was founded in 1958 and instruction of the Manitoba high school curriculum is offered for grades 7-12. Approximately 275 students attend Westgate and it is presently involved in a building program.[8] The school is run by twenty-six staff members who also teach religion, Mennonite history, choir and music.

Winnipeg Mennonite Elementary School

The Winnipeg Mennonite Elementary School was established in 1981 dedicated to providing high academic standards in a caring Christian environment. In 1988-89 there were 261 students taught by fifteen staff from kindergarten to grade six.[9] The school is located at 26 Columbus Crescent in a quiet suburban residential neighborhood in Westwood. It is supported by tuition, government grants and private donations. The school is inter-Mennonite and also includes non-Mennonite students from the community.

11

THE MEDIA AND
COMMUNICATIONS

Music making was an important part of the rural Mennonite churches, especially among the Russian Mennonites of the 1920s who allowed instruments and greater musical training. Since then Winnipeg has become a musical center. The same is true for the media. While Mennonite newspapers in early North America were often edited in small towns, these have been reestablished in urban centers, especially Winnipeg.

Urban Newspapers and Journals

Like the American Mennonite colleges and Canadian Bible schools, Mennonite newspapers and periodicals began in small towns. *Die Steinbach Post* began in Steinbach in 1913 and *Der Bote* in Rosthern in 1924. But Winnipeg has increasingly become an attractive center for the offices of periodicals, radio and television. Like Mennonite churches and institutions of higher education, there is a convergence of Mennonite media on Winnipeg.

In 1923 the publication of the two German language weeklies of the Mennonite Publishing House in Scottdale, Pennsylvania were transferred to Winnipeg. *Die Mennonitische Rundschau* and *Christlicher Jugendfreund* were the first urban Mennonite newspapers in Canada.[1]

This move seemed to be in anticipation of the coming of the large Mennonite immigration of the 1920s from Russia.

By 1940 the Rundschau Publishing House was reorganized into the Christian Press, now one of two Mennonite Brethren publishing agencies located in the MB Elmwood institutional center. In 1962 Rudy Wiebe became the first editor of the *Mennonite Brethren Herald*, the official English language newspaper of the Mennonite Brethren in Canada. It too is located in Elmwood.[2]

By the 1960s, *The Canadian Mennonite*, an inter-Mennonite weekly begun in 1953 by D.W. Friesen in Altona, Manitoba also moved its offices to Winnipeg on Donald Street. It folded in 1970 but *The Mennonite Reporter* soon followed as the national English Mennonite newspaper. It is still published in Waterloo, Ontario with a regional office in Winnipeg located at 1317A Portage Avenue. A cluster of offices are located here, including the monthly *Mennonite Mirror* and some of MCC's mediation and justice ministries.[3]

Winnipeg has continued to be an attractive center for Mennonite papers. The *Mennonite Mirror* began publishing in 1971. The editorial office of *The Mennonite*, the official periodical of the North American General Conference, was located in Winnipeg for fifteen years between 1971-86 (since relocated to Kansas). The editorial office of *Der Bote*, the General Conference Mennonite German language weekly, moved to Winnipeg in 1977 and is located on the CMBC campus. It is edited by Gerhard Ens. The EMMC editorial office moved to Winnipeg in 1980 when Henry Dueck was editor of *The Recorder*. Lyle Wahl, pastor of the St. Vital Community Church, became editor of the EMB *The Evangel* in 1985 so this periodical was also moved to Winnipeg.

The location of provincial, national and North American Mennonite papers in Winnipeg illustrates the influence of this urban center in the Mennonite communications world. The large population of Mennonites in the metropolis, its central location between Ontario and British Columbia where the majority of Canadian Mennonites live, the clustering of forty-seven Mennonite churches, and a number of national institutions have made Winnipeg an attractive center for Mennonite newspapers. Very few of the print and electronic media are located elsewhere in Canada, the *Mennonite Reporter* in Waterloo being one of the few exceptions.

Radio and Television Communications

While some of the more conservative rural Mennonites debated the merits or dangers of modern radio and television when they first arrived on the scene, by now there is little controversy over the use of these media. Indeed, Mennonites in Manitoba began radio broadcasting in the 1940s and their involvement in the electronic media has escalated with two studios and offices located in Winnipeg.

Just three years after the Mennonite Brethren began their college, some students aired their first English program over radio station CKRC in 1947, supported by a Gospel Light Hour quartet and choir. Today MB Communications' ministry has greatly increased. Its outreach programs involve English, High German, Russian and Low German radio broadcasts produced at its new building at 225 Riverton Avenue in Elmwood.

MB Communications is now engaged in seven major areas of electronic media programming. "*Licht des Evangeliums*" began in 1956. It is a half-hour weekly High German program broadcast over nine radio stations in Manitoba, Alberta, British Columbia, New York and Paraguay. The Low German program "*Licht vom Evangelium*" begun in 1959 is also a half-hour weekly program broadcast over seven stations in Ontario, the prairie provinces and Paraguay.[5] These German services include cassettes, video and film resources, church ministries and seminars.

The English "*Gospel Light Hour*" started in 1947. In 1957 Russian language programming was begun. Now three separate Russian programs are produced: a half-hour weekly program to Russian-speaking adults, a quarter-hour weekly program called "*Echo of Youth*" for Russian youth, and a fifteen minute weekly program in Russian in cooperation with Billy Graham's "Hour of Decision." These are released from Alaska, California, Ecuador, Guam, Saipan, the Philippines, Korea, Cyprus, Lebanon, Portugal and Monaco.[6]

A more recent English radio broadcast is "*Spin 180*," an hourly Sunday program of Christian rock music designed for youth. "The Third Story" is a half-hour English family television show, marketed in the five most westerly provinces from fifteen stations. It is a series production in magazine format for commercial and cable television.

Themes of the series include appetite, self, loneliness, persistence, despair, free will, fate, peers, values, thought, forgiveness and eternity.

The Conference of Mennonites in Canada has developed four major radio programs under Faith and Life Communications. They began broadcasting in 1957 when the Altona Mennonite radio station CFAM was launched. In 1969 the radio offices moved to Winnipeg and are now located at 1483 Pembina Highway. They plan to move to the CMBC campus in Tuxedo by 1990.[7]

The High German program "*Die Frohe Botschaft*" began in 1957 and is still broadcast over three stations in Manitoba and one South American station. The Low German program "*Wort des Lebens*" is also carried by the same stations for half an hour. The English program "*Abundant Life*" also started in 1957 broadcasting Sunday evenings, and occasional messages are printed for distribution four times a year.

The English program "*Faith and Life*" started in 1982 in a variety show format and is broadcast over three Manitoba stations on Sunday afternoons. George Wiebe and twenty singers organized the Faith and Life Male Choir which is an important feature of the broadcasts. The choir has recorded three tapes and in 1987 travelled widely in South America giving programs. Occasionally Faith and Life Communications provides speakers and guests for the CKY television program "*Sundayscope*," a half-hour national program which appears on Sundays.[8]

12

MUSIC AND THE ARTS

In the early 1920s a major circulation of the Mennonite saints took place on the prairies which helped to pave the way for the flowering of music and the arts. Thousands of rural Old Colony Mennonites moved to Mexico which opened up land for the Russian Mennonite immigrants in Manitoba and Saskatchewan. These Russian Mennonites had begun to develop their education and a taste for music and the arts, so they brought with them numerous leaders who had an enormous impact on these areas.

Choral Festivals and Workshops

Wesley Berg summarizes the work of five dedicated Mennonite music leaders: Franz Thiessen, K.H. Neufeld, John Konrad, David Paetkau and Ben Horch.[1] Thiessen, Konrad and Horch spent much of their time working in Winnipeg, and Neufeld organized several major festivals in the city. All five were born in Russia, although Horch grew up in Winnipeg. Thiessen and Neufeld working out of Rosthern and Winkler respectively prepared the ground in rural Mennonite churches by conducting large mass music festivals, introducing choral and classical music often accompanied by orchestras.[2] This emphasis on "Kunst" or musical performance at higher levels of sophistication was not immediately accepted but required prolonged teaching and development.

Franz Thiessen was in Winnipeg during 1932-43, where he conducted the choir at the North End MB Church, and performed great works such as Mendelssohn's *St. Paul*. John Konrad had come to Winnipeg from Winkler a year earlier in 1931 where for fifteen years he conducted the choir at First Mennonite Church. Thus, two of the three Mennonite churches in the city were blessed with some of the best choral musicians in the country. Konrad focused most of his efforts on teaching instrumental music, especially the violin. He was put in charge of the string section of the Winnipeg Bornoff School of Music in 1942, which he bought in 1950 and continued as the Konrad Conservatory.[3] Konrad was a pioneer in developing stringed instrumental performances. His choral performances always included an orchestra performing Mendelssohn's *Elijah* and especially Carl Loewe's *Das Suehnopfer des Neuen Bundes* which was performed annually.[4] When the Canadian Mennonite Bible College began in 1947 Konrad was its music and choir leader for several years. Since they were contemporaries, Thiessen, Konrad and Neufeld occasionally combined their efforts at choral seminars and performances. In 1945 Neufeld and Konrad held the largest festival with a mass choir of 800 singers and a thirty-piece orchestra in the Winnipeg Auditorium where 4,500 persons listened.[5]

Ben Horch, born of Lutheran parents, came to Winnipeg from Russia as an infant and grew up in a musical home. His parents later joined the North End MB Church. He began conducting at the Winnipeg Bible College where he taught music, and conducted at the church as well as being involved in music seminars.[6]

When MBBC began in 1944, Ben and Esther Horch were appointed to the music department. Here Ben developed his *Kernleider*, an attempt at linking the religious pietism of the Mennonite Brethren and more rational classical music. Later he left the college to work in the music department of the Canadian Broadcasting Corporation for fourteen years.[7] "*Hymn Sing*," a half-hour national weekly TV program of singing, was one of his dreams come true.

Flowering of Mennonite Music in Winnipeg

These five major music leaders laid the groundwork for an explosion of Mennonite musical talent which after the 1940s centered around the three educational institutions of MBBC, CMBC and the University of

Manitoba. This reservoir of musical acceptance and talent has allowed many recent Mennonite musicians to gain influence far beyond the borders of Winnipeg.

In 1954 George and Esther Wiebe were appointed to head the music department at CMBC.[8] The college students provided George with the opportunity to conduct one or more choirs. Now the need for choral festivals across Canada is more focused on the two Winnipeg colleges where music students study. They have fanned out across Canada from both Mennonite colleges as church choir directors, vocalists and singers. These two colleges have combined their choirs for the last twenty-five years, so mass choirs have performed major classical works at the Winnipeg Centennial Concert Hall annually with college conductors taking turns. Two very major recent week-long training sessions brought the renowned Robert Shaw and Helmuth Rilling to Winnipeg as Visiting Conductors. Esther Wiebe has taught music at CMBC for more than 25 years and has been a major reason for the success of the program. She has become one of the best known Mennonite composers and publisher of music in Canada. In 1973 she composed the folk opera *The Bridge* which was put on stage. Between 1975 and 1987 she published a series of four arrangements and compositions for choirs, and in 1984 she and Urie Bender published the cantata *That They May Be One*.[9] The Wiebes have worked as a team in most performances.

Similar musical performances and training have occurred at MBBC spearheaded by William and Irmgard Baerg.[10] The joint MBBC and CMBC performances started by the Wiebes and Victor Martens (who preceeded the Baergs) have continued. For many years William conducted the Winnipeg Singers which have since become the CBC Singers, and he has always been involved in guest conducting and adjudication at various festivals. Irmgard is a professional pianist often playing for her husband's choirs, but also is engaged in various performances. John Martens is on the music faculty at MBBC, concentrating on voice instruction, performances at various concerts as a tenor soloist, and director of the Winnipeg Singers.

Henry Engbrecht came to Winnipeg from Winkler to become the music director and conductor of the Winnipeg Philharmonic Choir in 1975. In 1988-89 they performed with the Winnipeg Philharmonic Orchestra doing works by Puccini, Robinovitch and Beethoven.[11]

Engbrecht is on the faculty of the School of Music at the University of Manitoba where he teaches and conducts the University Singers, performing works such as Brahms, Schumann and Rossini in 1989.

There are numerous other musical activities. There is the forty-voice Winnipeg Mennonite Children's Choir founded in 1957 and directed by Helen Litz, which has travelled all over the world, winning prizes in Europe and North America.[12] Prairie Performances, Manitoba Inc. was founded in 1987 dedicated to performance opportunities of artists in Winnipeg. Judge John Enns is the president and two-thirds of their Board and Council are Mennonite.[13] With forty-seven Mennonite churches in Winnipeg there are hundreds of musicians and performers who cannot be mentioned here. In 1968 Arnold Schellenberg made a study of one hundred Mennonite musicians in the city assessing their training, group participation, experience and versatility. He found that Mennonites are involved in the whole range of musical endeavor.[14] In the 1989 Winnipeg Competition Music Festival (held annually) there were twenty-two Mennonites who made it into the finals.

Early Mennonite Writers and Poets

It is clear in our discussion of Mennonite work, education, health care and service that there has been a change from in-group concerns with rural survival to entering the larger society and the challenges it holds. Nowhere is this change more evident than in writing and the arts. Let us trace this progression of interest from the lost Russian *Heimat*, or homeland, to the pioneer setting of the rural Canadian community, and finally the transfer of interest to the larger society and the world. Gordon Childe has suggested one of the indicators of urbanization is the development of novels, poetry, art and theater. Winnipeg Mennonites have entered the world of the arts and changes in their world outlook are clearly evident.

While the early Mennonites of the 1870s were untrained and considered creative writing "worldly," some of the Russian Mennonites had studied in the schools and universities of western Europe. There are two major waves of Mennonite writers in Winnipeg representing the pre and post-World War II periods. Arnold Dyck was the most notable writer of the first period and Rudy Wiebe of the second, both of whom lived in

Winnipeg for some time.[15]

Arnold Dyck, the undisputed pioneer in Canadian Mennonite writing, studied literature and art in Munich, Dresden and St. Petersburg before arriving in Steinbach, Manitoba in 1923. He edited a newspaper, managed a press, founded a literary journal and created the *Echo Verlag*.[16] He is best known, however, for his many writings in High and Low German. In the early 1940s he moved to the North Kildonan Mennonite enclave where he spent twenty years (with short trips to Germany) well into the latter 1960s. In Winnipeg he completed his autobiographical High German novel *Verloren in der Steppe* which appeared in five slender volumes between 1944 and 1948.[17] He also wrote most of his Low German *Koop enn Bua* booklet series in Winnipeg.[18] In his autobiography *Aus Meinem Leben*, he writes that between 1944 and 1960 he published seventeen 100-page booklets, eleven in Low German and six in High German.[19] The *Verloren in der Steppe* series was based on Mennonite life in Russia, while the *Koop enn Bua* series dealt with Mennonite rural life in Canada.

Recently Victor Doerksen, George Epp, Harry Loewen, Elizabeth Peters and Al Reimer, scholars at the Universities of Manitoba and Winnipeg, edited all of Dyck's writings into four thick volumes known as the *Collected Works: Arnold Dyck* published and to be published between 1985 and 1990.[20] Dyck's works have clearly stimulated other efforts as well. Al Reimer's novel *My Harp is Turned to Mourning* is focused on the Russian Mennonite experience between 1905 and 1924 just before they came to Winnipeg. Reimer has also been involved in translating novels by Dietrich Neufeld, *A Russian Dance of Death*, and Hans Harder's *No Strangers in Exile*, both of which deal with the difficult Mennonite experiences in Russia in the 1920s and 1930s.[21]

A series of anthologies and collections of poems and short writings were published by Mennonite Winnipeggers in the seventies and eighties. William DeFehr and others published the collection *Harvest* (1974), and George Epp published the German anthology *Unter dem Nordlicht* (1977). Harry Loewen's *Mennonite Images* (1980) dealt with historical, cultural and literary Mennonite essays mostly in English; Al Reimer and Jack Thiessen collected *A Sackful of Plautdietsch* (1983) written in Low German; and Harry Loewen and Al Reimer published *Visions and Realities* (1985) while Victor Doerksen focused on writer

Gerhard J. Friesen in *Fritz Senn* (1987).[22]

Recent Novelists and Poets

Rudy Wiebe represents the newer Canadian generation of writers following World War II. Wiebe became the first editor of the new *Mennonite Brethren Herald* in 1962, the same year his first novel *Peace Shall Destroy Many* was published. The focus was on a Mennonite pioneer community in Saskatchewan and its struggles on the prairies in 1944. The controversy over the novel resulted in Wiebe's resignation from the editorship of the *MB Herald* so his stay in Winnipeg was very brief. Since then he has written twenty novels and many collections of short stories.[23] While Wiebe's first novels dealt with Mennonite rural foibles and problems, he soon branched out into problems of other minorities. More recently his novel *My Lovely Enemy* takes place in the city dealing with the pressures of professional life in the university. Similar trends of change are beginning to show in the works of other Mennonite writers. As Mennonites move from the rural community enclave into the city, they need to work through their early socialization and community demands, followed by the opportunities of greater freedom and individualism of urban life.

There are a variety of younger writers such as Patrick Friesen, Menno Wiebe, David Waltner-Toews, Clinton Toews, Di Brandt, Audrey Poettker, Lois Braun and Sandra Birdsell who are coming out with poetry and stories. Pat Friesen has at least five collections of poems including *The Lands I Am, Bluebottle* (1978), *The Shunning* (1980), *Unearthly Horses* (1984), and *Flicker and Hawk* (1987).[24] Like Rudy Wiebe's novels, Friesen's early books of poems focus much on rural Mennonite themes; *The Shunning*, which has been adapted for the stage and performed successfully, deals with the pressures of rural Mennonite life. More recently his poems are less ethnic and community oriented but deal with themes of individual freedom and inspiration. The need to work through conservative Mennonite pressures are especially evident in Di Brandt's first collection of poems titled *Questions I Asked My Mother* (1987).[25] Brandt has been nominated for several Canadian awards in poetry and she has read her works abroad. She is presently completing her Ph.D. in English.

David Waltner-Toews grew up in Winnipeg as one of the first "city" Mennonites, and he appears less in need of digesting his past in his four volumes.[26] He seems to have integrated Mennonite beliefs, food, culture and life, so he was able to deal with universal themes sooner. There are increasingly more second generation Mennonites who may have less ethnic agenda to deal with and be able to set a faster pace of integration. To what extent these new poets and writers will retain their Mennonite identity or assimilate will be interesting to observe. Some of the writers we have discussed would identify themselves as Mennonite more than others.

Winnipeg Mennonite Theater

In 1971 Paul Neustaedter, Gerd Neuendorff and John J. Enns organized the Winnipeg Mennonite Theater which performed its first production in 1972. In the first ten years the organization raised its curtain on some seventy-five performances including ten mainstage plays, seventeen one-act plays, four operas, two short musical sketches, a staged secular cantata, two "composer" evenings of *lieder*, and an evening of folksongs and readings.[27] These performances included comedies, tragedies, documentary-style presentations, classic and modern, historical and eight performances of a Christian religious nature. A majority of the Board of Directors have been Mennonite, and plays have been performed in both German and English.

The theater has continued since 1982 with operas, plays, comedies, stage and one-act plays, tragedies, musicals, solos and folksongs.[28] Funding has come from the Manitoba Ethnic Cultural Society, Winnipeg Foundation and private donors.

It is interesting to see the progression of Mennonite involvement in which they were able to compete for grants from the Manitoba Arts Council during the five-year span of 1983 to 1988.[29] During this five-year period sixty Mennonites (mostly from Winnipeg) received grants in music; twenty-one in the literary arts, twelve in the visual arts, seven in theater but none in dance. The number of grants in each area has also more than doubled, so Mennonites are increasingly asking for support.[30] Well over half of all grants were received in music where Mennonites have always been strong; as yet they do not appear to be involved in dance which in the past was considered taboo. Mennonites in Winnipeg are clearly engaged in music and the arts, and their focus is moving from the ethnic and sacred to include a variety of classical and modern expressions in the arts.

**Robert Shaw conducting Mass Mennonite Choir in Winnipeg
Concert Hall at a Music workshop
sponsored by the Mennonite Colleges.
(Photo: Robert Nickel)**

13

SERVICE AND OUTREACH

Mennonites have also reached out to the needs of others. This outreach has taken many forms involving a variety of agencies, many of them located in Winnipeg.

Mennonite Central Committee Canada

The Mennonite Central Committee (MCC) began in 1920 when Mennonites in North America assisted their kin in Russia who had suffered through the Revolution and famine. Food and clothing was sent with emissaries as relief in "The Name of Christ. " A variety of relief and peace organizations emerged in many parts of Canada which all sent their gifts to the MCC headquarters located in Akron, Pennsylvania. After World War II these relief efforts coordinated by MCC involved service to Mennonites and others. The varieties of service expanded into many regional, often fragmented and isolated relief organizations in Canada which were not as effective as they might have been.

In December 1963 a single Canadian, inter-Mennonite relief and service agency, the Mennonite Central Committee Canada (MCCC), was formed.[1] Its central offices were located in Winnipeg, first downtown on Princess Street, later on Pembina Highway, and most recently at 134 Plaza Drive in a new building in the southern end of Winnipeg.

MCC Canada is the Canadian arm of the larger international Mennonite Central Committee which has more than 1,000 people working in fifty countries on all continents of the world. While originally MCC was involved almost entirely in providing food and clothing as relief, more recently it has become increasingly involved in development programs. Relief and material aid help to keep people alive, while development programs are designed to help people help themselves, providing assistance in agricultural development, aid to develop schools, hospitals, small businesses and the like. While MCC mainly used to work with Mennonites, now the majority of MCC programs deal with others who are not Mennonite.

There are forty people working in the Winnipeg offices, administering a 1989 budget of some $19,000,000.[2] Overseas programs involve immigration services, food concerns, East-West relations, service education, trainee exchanges, child sponsorship, handicapped concerns, China Educational Exchange and food services related to Africa. Canadian programs include services in employment, native concerns, disabled people's concerns, mental health and operation of the Ottawa office. All these programs are supported by personnel, financial and information services. In 1989 MCC Canada, together with the provincial MCCs, celebrated its twenty-fifth anniversary.

Mennonite Central Committee Manitoba

When MCC Canada was organized in 1963, five provincial MCCs were also set up in Ontario, Manitoba, Saskatchewan, Alberta and British Columbia in 1964 (Alberta in 1965).[3] These provincial offices work at the grassroots level, in contact with the provincial churches, institutions and organizations recruiting volunteers, collecting funds and material aid. MCC Manitoba is also located in Winnipeg at 134 Plaza Drive, with a staff of about twenty-five to thirty persons. At an annual meeting some 600 delegates and members plan for the year. Meetings occur approximately every other year in one of the forty-seven Mennonite churches in Winnipeg, and on alternate years in small towns and cities in rural Manitoba.

MCC Manitoba is involved in gathering material aid such as soap, clothes, blankets, layettes and school supplies which are sent overseas. Refugee assistance, ministry to farmers, family services, voluntary service, justice ministries, self-help crafts and thrift stores are part of its programs. The ministry to Mexico Mennonites returning to Canada is located in Winkler and the El Dad ministry to handicapped offenders is located in St. Giroux.

Dedication of the new Mennonite Central Committee building in Winnipeg, 1986.
(Photo: Bruce Hildebreand of MCC Canada)

Mediation and Justice Services

MCC Manitoba also has five people working with Mediation Services located at 205-1317A Portage Avenue. The program which provides peacemaking and conflict resolution in the community through mediation began in 1979. It works primarily within the criminal justice system with the approval and cooperation of the police department and Attorney General of Manitoba. Offender and victim meet together with an impartial third party to resolve their conflict in an acceptable way to both parties. These conflicts involve criminal charges such as assault, mischief, threats, conflicts between neighbors or friends, disagreements between landlords and tenants, coworkers or family members.[4] It provides both victim and offender the opportunity to get directly involved in resolutions. In 1987 800 cases were referred to Mediation Services, and 270 cases were successfully mediated.

Open Circle is another part of Mediation Services. In 1988 one MCC Manitoba staff person and forty-four volunteers worked with fifty male inmates at the federal maximum security prison at Stoney Mountain Penitentiary, the provincial correctional institution at Headingley, the Rockwood minimum security farm, and the correctional institution at Portage la Prairie. Volunteers visit these inmates regularly. Many of these men never receive any visits. Stoney Mountain Penitentiary and Rockwood are located fifteen kilometers north of Winnipeg, and Headingley is located fifteen kilometers west of Winnipeg. Many MCC voluntary service workers have also served at Winnipeg's Marymound Correctional Center for Girls.

MCC Thrift and Gift Shops

The story of MCC thrift shops began in 1972 when the material aid program changed direction, and clothing for refugees and victims of war were no longer needed overseas. Four Mennonite women in Altona, Manitoba opened up a self-help center in March of 1972 to convert used and new articles into cash, provide quality clothing and other items for the community at reasonable prices, promote inter-Mennonite relations and create a sales outlet for MCC self-help crafts.[5] A few months later, two thrift shops were opened in Winnipeg on the east and west sides of the Red River, one located at 447 Watt Street and the other at 859 Sargent Avenue. Used clothes and items are brought to these stores and sold to customers who need good inexpensive clothing. During the past years the Sargent Avenue store has annually generated incomes in the $55-60,000 range, most of which is turned over to the MCC Manitoba for relief and services overseas.[6] Literally hundreds of volunteers have been involved in this service.

Some of these stores also sell self-help crafts which are imported from those countries of the world where MCC works. The largest self-help store is located at the main offices on 134 Plaza Drive with total sales of $275,000 during 1987-88. Olive Branch Gift Shop, located at 185 Henderson Highway, sold self-help products amounting to $92,000 the same year. These stores are run mostly by volunteers and sell crafts produced in India, the Philippines, Bangladesh, Thailand, Haiti, Vietnam, El Salvador, Pakistan and other countries. Crafts are made for a going wage so it is a means of providing jobs for the unemployed in these countries.

Canadian Foodgrains Bank

The Canadian Foodgrains Bank located at 400-280 Smith Street specializes in shipping Canadian grain to places of the world which are in need. Farmers donate grain, others donate cash for shipping, and the Canadian International Development Agency (CIDA) provides millions of dollars to support the program. In 1989 there were seven cooperating organizations including the Canadian Baptist Federation, Canadian Lutheran World Relief, Christian and Missionary Alliance, Christian Reformed World Relief, Mennonite Central Committee Canada, Pentecostal Assemblies of Canada and United Church of Canada. The Foodgrains Bank idea began in 1975 with MCC Canada and was expanded to include other participants in 1983. By 1987 the bank had shipped a total of 185,600 metric tonnes of grain to twenty Third World countries consisting mostly of wheat contributed by Canadian farmers.[7] Ethiopia, Mozambique, the Sudan, Algeria, India and Nicaragua were some of the major recipients. In 1989 the MCC Canada budget included $5.5 million for the Foodgrains Bank (including CIDA funds).

Mennonite Economic Development Association

In 1953 eight Mennonite businessmen met in Chicago to begin the Mennonite Economic Development Association (MEDA) to help Paraguayan entrepreneurs become economically self-sufficient. By 1978 MEDA's programs extended to twenty-five countries on five continents. Its aim is to improve production/marketing projects, small business development programs and human resource services such as consulting. In 1987 there were 1,651 members and total revenues were $1,226,441 (US).[8] Economic development work is done mostly in Jamaica, Haiti, Bolivia, Belize and Paraguay. The Canadian MEDA offices are located at 402-280 Smith Street.

Crossroads Family Center

In 1973 this center was established in the Winnipeg core area at 211 Isabel which is supported by five Mennonite churches and the Core Area Development Fund. Originally it was a drop-in center for low income mothers with pre-schoolers who needed help and friends. It has now developed into a family center where mothers learn cooking and sew crafts, men and women are assisted with finding employment, and children enjoy activities. Two hired staff and numerous volunteers run the center. Mennonites are also deeply involved in the Agape Table located at Home Street Mennonite Church which provides meals for the poor.

14

WINNIPEG MENNONITES IN THE CANADIAN SETTING

Before World War II Mennonites in Canada were largely rural, but they began to move to small towns. However, after the 1940s, there was an important shift toward larger cities, including Winnipeg. By 1981 the majority were urban (51.4 percent).[1] Thus the 1970s were the watershed between rural Mennonite dominance and the beginnings of greater urban influence.

The Rural-Urban Shift

In 1941, ninety-one percent of all Mennonites in Canada were rural, most being farmers. Only one out of eleven Mennonites was a city dweller. Today there are twice as many urban Mennonites in Winnipeg alone (19,105 in 1981) as there were in all of Canada in 1941 (9,446). Such enormous demographic shifts have profound impacts on style of life, because Mennonites began entering new occupations. Their upward social mobility, higher education and income would affect beliefs and attitudes which resulted in a new way of life.

In 1941 about one-half (5,147 or fifty-five percent) of the 9,446 urban Mennonites lived in large metropolitan areas of 100,000 plus. Almost one-third of these lived in Kitchener-Waterloo (1,472) and one-fourth in Winnipeg (1,285).[2] By 1951 the Winnipeg Mennonite population had tripled in a decade, and another decade later it had quad-rupled again, so that by 1961 the Winnipeg population had multiplied more than ten times in twenty years to 13,595. Winnipeg emerged as the largest center of Mennonites in Canada, and very soon it became the largest concentration of urban Mennonites in the world. While the Kitchener-Waterloo Mennonite population tripled during the two decades (1941-61) from 1,472 to 4,480, the Vancouver Mennonite population increased ten-fold to become the second largest (5,260) concentration of Canadian Mennonites in 1961. We can think of these three centers as the metro Mennonite "Big Three."

As shown in Table 1, there are many additional metropolitan areas in 1981 including St. Catharines, Saskatoon, Calgary, Toronto and Edmonton, which all count 2,000 Mennonites or more. It is interesting to note the five largest Mennonite metros are also located in the five largest Mennonite settlements in the Niagara and Ontario Peninsula, and the Red, Fraser and Saskatchewan River valleys. Each of them has a substantial rural Mennonite supporting population. The Calgary, Toronto and Edmonton Mennonite rural populations are smaller, and the rest have few rural Mennonites to draw from.

To place all these numbers into a model we have plotted the Canadian metropolitan areas in Table 2. Demographically, Winnipeg in 1989 is clearly in the center, with the older Kitchener-Waterloo in the East, supported by eastern St. Catharines and Toronto, and the younger Vancouver in the West, flanked by cities like Saskatoon, Edmonton and Calgary.

Table 1: Mennonite Population in Canadian Metropolitan Areas (100,000 plus).

Metro Centers	Mennonite Population					Total 1981 Metropolitan Population
	1941	1951	1961	1971	1981	
Winnipeg	1,285	3,460	13,595	17,850	19,105	585,000
Kitch/Water.	1,472	1,646	4,480	5,235	9,760	288,000
Vancouver	559	1,624	5,260	8,880	9,515	1,268,000
St. Catharines	200	510	2,515	5,955	5,985	304,000
Saskatoon	871	1,663	4,765	5,697	5,380	154,000
Calgary	91	233	1,220	2,650	3,635	593,000
Toronto	326	267	1,375	2,540	2,950	2,999,000
Edmonton	29	85	455	1,590	1,920	657,000
Montreal	54	65	140	580	750	2,828,000
Regina	87	90	240	520	685	164,000
London	13	45	115	645	485	284,000
Hamilton	41	66	250	425	420	542,000
Victoria	10	14	45	145	320	233,000
Ottawa-Hull	12	28	60	230	285	693,000
Windsor	62	49	85	210		246,000
Sudbury	13	7	55	160		150,000
Thunder Bay	22	13	34	70		121,000
Halifax		1	7	40		278,000
Quebec		1	0	20		576,000
St. John's			9	10		155,000
Saint John		16	1	5		114,000
Oshawa						154,000
Chicoutimi				5		135,000
Trois Rivieres						111,000
Totals	5,147	9,888	34,706	53,462	61,195	13,632,000

Sources: 1941, 1951, 1961, 1971 and 1981 Census of Canada Catalogues.

Mennonite Churches in Metro Canada

There are twenty-four metropolitan areas in Canada and Mennonites have established 137 churches in fourteen of these large urban centers. Table 2 shows that only twenty Mennonite churches were located in six metropolitan areas before 1940, and 118 after World War II.[3] Between twenty-two and twenty-six churches were established in each of the decades of the fifties, sixties and seventies, and forty-one were established in the eighties. The explosion of Mennonite church planting began after World War II and it seems to be escalating again. The Mennonite metropolitan adult church membership in 1988 was 25,223 and there were 61,195 including unbaptized youth and children in 1981.

To further illustrate the dominance of Winnipeg Mennonites in Canada, we see one-third of metro Mennonite churches are located in Winnipeg (forty-seven out of 140). More than one-third of the metro Mennonite members are also located in Winnipeg (9,352 out of 25,223). The central location in Canada as well as its very large rural reserves have all combined to add to Winnipeg's Mennonite growth. Indeed, since the 1940s from seven to fifteen new churches have been planted in each of the last four decades. This demographic Mennonite mass has added greatly to the vibrance of this religious urban community.

From our study it is clear, however, that enormous changes are taking place in worship, work, education, communications and outreach. While Mennonites have existed in Winnipeg for more than seventy-five years, in comparison to Mennonites in Amsterdam they have only begun. It will be interesting to see how they will change and adjust in the future. The struggle to redefine their identity is evident in their literature, work, worship and communications.

Table 2. Mennonite Churches and Membership in Canadian Metropolitan Centers.

Metro Centers	Churches Established in								Mennonite Churches	Mennonite Church Membership 1988	Mennonites 1981 Census
	Pre-1920	20s	30s	40s	50s	60s	70s	80s			
Winnipeg	1	2	1	2	8	11	7	15	47	9,352	19,105
Vancouver			2	2	3	5	6	6	24	4,780	9,515
Kitchener/Waterloo	3	3			1	1		3	11	2,725	9,760
Saskatoon				2	4	3	1	4	14	2,565	5,380
St. Catharines	1		3	1	1	1			7	2,180	5,985
Calgary			1	1	2		2	3	9	1,193	3,635
Toronto	2						3	5	10	826	2,950
Edmonton					2	1	1	2	6	654	1,920
Montreal						1	1		2	200	750
Regina				1		1		1	3	366	685
London											485
Hamilton					1	1	1		3	170	420
Victoria							1		1	48	320
Ottawa						1		1	2	139	285
Quebec								1	1	25	
Totals	7	5	7	9	22	26	23	41	140	25,223	61,195

Sources: Frank Epp, Mennonites in Canada, Volume 2, 1982, pp.269-89; 1988 Survey of Metropolitan Mennonite Churches by the author; 1981 Census of Canada.

WINNIPEG MENNONITE CONGREGATIONS

Information - Courtesy of Mennonite Heritage Centre

WINNIPEG MENNONITE CONGREGATIONS

1. Christian Fellowship Chapel EMB
   465 Osborne St.
2. St. Vital Community Church EMB
   11 Avalon Rd.
3. Aberdeen EMC
   537 Aberdeen Ave.
4. Braeside EMC
   1011 Munroe
5. Crestview Fellowship EMC
   271 Hamilton
6. Fort Garry EMC
   602 Pasadena
7. Gospel Mennonite EMMC
   232 Nassua St.
8. Morrow Gospel EMMC
   Lot 128, St. Anne's Rd.
9. Bethel Mennonite
   870 Carter Ave.
10. Burrows Bethel
    Burrows & Charles
11. Charleswood Mennonite
    669 Haney St.
12. Douglas Ave. Mennonite
    1417 Rothesay St.
13. First Mennonite
    922 Notre Dame Ave.
14. Fort Garry Mennonite
    150 Bayridge
14. Home Street Mennonite
    318 Home St.
16. North Kildonan Mennonite
    1131 Roch St.
17. Northdale Mennonite
    19 Pinecrest Bay
18. Sargent Ave. Mennonite
    926 Garfield St.
19. Springfield Heights Mennonite
    570 Sharron Bay
20. Sterling Mennonite
    1008 Dakota
21. Winnipeg Chinese Mennonite
    1010 Riverwood Ave.
22. Brooklands Community MB
    44 Tentler St.
23. Elmwood MB
    145 Henderson Highway
24. Fort Garry MB
    1771 Pembina Highway
25. Maples MB
    1192 Jefferson
26. McIvor Ave. MB
    200 McIvor Ave.
27. North Kildonan MB
    217 Kingsford Ave.
28. Portage Ave. MB
    1420 Portage Ave.
29. River East MB
    755 McLeod Ave.
30. Salem MB
    691 Alexander Ave.
31. Westwood Community MB
    401 Westwood
32. Winnipeg Central MB
    520 Williams Ave.
33. Transcona Community MB
    228 Dowling Ave. West
*34. Church of the Open Door
    137 Euclid
35. Sommerfeld Mennonite
    345 Simcoe St.
36. Erin St. Mission Chapel (Chortizer)
    1344 Erin St.
*37. Grain of Wheat Church Community
    232 Home St.
38. L'Eglise Chretienne Evang. De. St. Boniface MB
    231 Kitson
39. Cornerstone Christian Fellowship MB
    700 Notre Dame Ave.
40. Hope Mennonite Church
    86 Westgate
41. Iglesia Cristiana de Habla Hispana MB
    145 Henderson Highway
42. Native Church Planting MB
    764 Stewart St.
43. Portuguese MB
    169 Riverton ave.
44. Richmond Gospel Fellowship EMMC
    99 Killarney
45. St. Vital MB
    485 Meadowwood
46. Valley Gardens Community Church MB
    220 Antrim Ave.
47. Winnipeg Chinese MB
    520 William

* Related Groups

REFERENCES

CHAPTER 1

    1. Frank Epp, <u>Mennonites in Canada, 1786-1920: The History of a Separate People</u> (Toronto: Macmillan of Canada, 1974), p. 201.

    2. Hudson's Bay Company Archives, Provincial Archives of Manitoba, Winnipeg.

    3. Alan F.J. Artibise, <u>Winnipeg: A Social History of Urban Growth, 1874-1914</u> (Montreal: McGill-Queen's University Press, 1975), p. 9.

    4. G.F.G. Stanley, <u>Louis Riel: Rebel of the Western Frontier or Victim of Politics and Prejudice?</u> (Toronto: Copp Clark, 1969).

    5. Artibise, <u>Winnipeg</u>, p. 9.

    6. Artibise, <u>Winnipeg</u>, p. 5.

    7. W.L. Morton, <u>Manitoba: A History</u> (Toronto: 1957), p. 166.

    8. Epp, <u>Mennonites in Canada</u>, Vol.1, p. 200.

    9. J. Steen and W. Bryce, <u>Winnipeg, Manitoba and Her Industries</u> (Winnipeg: 1882), p. 11.

    10. Artibise, <u>Winnipeg</u>, p. 14.

    11. E.K. Francis, <u>In Search of Utopia: Mennonites in Manitoba</u> (Altona: D.W. Friesen and Sons, 1955), p. 28.

    12. Francis, <u>Utopia</u>, p. 50.

    13. Epp, <u>Mennonites in Canada</u>, Vol.1, p. 212.

CHAPTER 2

    1. Artibise, <u>Winnipeg</u>, p. 159.

    2. Artibise, <u>Winnipeg</u>, p. 159.

    3. Artibise, <u>Winnipeg</u>, p. 161.

    4. Anna Thiessen, <u>Die Stadtmission in Winnipeg</u> (Winnipeg: Regier Printing, 1955), p. 7.

    5. Thiessen, <u>Stadtmission</u>, p. 8.

    6. Thiessen, <u>Stadtmission</u>, pp. 5-10.

    7. Interview with Esther and Ben Horch at 1118 Rothesay, Winnipeg in their home. The author and the Horchs spent a morning driving around in the North End to the historic places.

    8. Thiessen, <u>Stadtmission</u>, p. 24.

CHAPTER 3

    1. Esther Horch, <u>C.N. Hiebert Was My Father</u> (Winnipeg: Christian Press, 1979), p. 19.

    2. Thiessen, <u>Stadtmission</u>, p. 32.

    3. Thiessen, <u>Stadtmission</u>, pp. 47-70.

    4. Thiessen, <u>Stadtmission</u>, pp. 47-100. Thiessen has written a number of books and pamphlets: "Die Entstehung und Entwicklung der Mennoniten Brüder Gemeinde in Winnipeg, 1907-1966," unpublished manuscript, 1966; "Kurzer Bericht: Maria Martha Heim," undated; Marlene Epp, "The Mennonite Girls' Homes of Winnipeg (1925-1959): A Home Away From Home," <u>Journal of Mennonite Studies</u> 6, 1988.

    5. Thiessen, <u>Stadtmission</u>, p. 47.

    6. Thiessen, <u>Stadtmission</u>, pp. 49-51.

    7. Eric Rempel, "Eben Ezer Girls' Homes: Winnipeg (1926-59)," unpublished paper, (CMBC April 1977), p. 1.

    8. Rempel, "Eben Ezer," pp. 6-7.

    9. Epp, "Girls' Homes," pp. 1-25.

    10. Frank H. Epp, "Mennonitische Rundshau (1978-1956)," <u>Mennonite Historical Bulletin</u>, Volume 17, Number 4 (October 1956), pp. 1-3.

11. J.H. Enns, Dem Herrn die Ehre: Schönwieser Mennoniten Gemeinde von Manitoba (Altona: D.W. Friesen and Sons, 1969), pp. 67-68.

12. Thiessen, Stadtmission, pp. 113-5.

CHAPTER 4

1. Herbert Neufeld, "Early Settlement of North Kildonan," in Fiftieth Anniversary of the Mennonite Settlement in North Kildonan, Ed. Karl Fast (Winnipeg: North Kildonan Mennonite Churches, 1978), pp. 16-17.

2. D. Klassen, "The Establishment of the North Kildonan Mennonite Settlement," in Fiftieth Anniversary of the Mennonite Settlement in North Kildonan, p. 30.

3. Klassen, "Settlement," pp. 33-35.

4. Klassen, "Settlement," pp. 34-35.

5. Karl Fast, in "The 25th Anniversary of the Mennonite Settlement of North Kildonan," Fiftieth Anniversary of the Mennonite Settlement in North Kildonan, p. 40.

6. Fast, "25th Anniversary," pp. 38-49.

7. Carl Driedger, "The Formation and Growth of the North Kildonan Mennonite Church," in Fiftieth Anniversary of the Mennonite Settlement in North Kildonan, p. 78.

8. Herb Kopp, "The Mennonite Brethren Church in Canada: A Century of Grace," Mennonite Brethren Herald, Volume 27, Number 11 (May 1988), p. 43.

9. Kopp, "Century," pp. 42-46.

10. Driedger, "North Kildonan," pp. 78-80.

11. Bill Schultz, ed., 50th Anniversary, North Kildonan Mennonite Church, 1935-1985 (Altona: D.W. Friesen and Sons, 1985), pp. 10-15.

12. Mary Funk, "A History of the Northdale Mennonite Fellowship," in Fiftieth Anniversary of the Mennonite Settlement in North Kildonan, pp.99-102.

CHAPTER 5

1. John A. Toews, A History of the Mennonite Brethren Church (Hillsboro, Kansas: Mennonite Brethren Publishing, 1975), pp. 276-9.

2. Toews, MB History, p. 267.

3. Erich Ratzlaff, "Ein Ehrwurdiges Alter," Mennonitische Rundschau, Volume 100, Number 27 (1977), pp. 1-3.

4. Toews, MB History, pp. 291-4.

5. Toews, MB History, p. 320.

6. The author spent considerable time in the MB archives located in the Elmwood area and interviewed Ken Reddig.

CHAPTER 6

1. Henry J. Gerbrandt, "The Mennonite Scene Before Bethel," in Bethel Pioneering in Faith, 1937-1987 Ed. Betty Dyck (Altona: D.W. Friesen and Sons, 1988), p. 9.

2. Gerbrandt, "Bethel," p. 11.

3. Gerbrandt, "Bethel," p. 12.

4. Gerbrandt, "Bethel," pp. 9-14.

5. Gerbrandt, "Bethel," p. 14.

6. Gerbrandt, "Bethel," p. 27. I also interviewed David Schroeder, a former pastor of Bethel.

7. Lee Toews, "Evangelical Mennonite Church: Beginnings in Winnipeg," in Celebrating God's Faithfulness, 1950s to 1980s (Steinbach: Derksen Printers, 1986), p. 4.

8. Toews, "EMC," pp. 1-40.

9. Toews, "EMC," pp. 1-40.

10. Dennis Stoesz, The Story of Home Street Mennonite Church 1957-1982: Responses to the Urban Environment (Steinbach: Derksen Printers, 1985), p.5.

11. Stoesz, Home Street Mennonite, pp. 25-27.

12. Jack Heppner, Search for Renewal: The Story of the Rudnerweider/EMMC, 1937-1987 (Altona: D.W. Friesen and Sons, 1987), pp. 39-43.

13. Heppner, EMMC, pp. 162-5, 181-2, 192-4.

14. Interview with Gladys Penner, office secretary at the EMMC conference office at 526 Macmillan Avenue, Winnipeg.

CHAPTER 7

1. Gibson Winter, The Suburban Captivity of the Churches (New York: Macmillan, 1962).

2. Winter, Captivity, pp. 1-50.

3. Artibise, Winnipeg, pp. 1-50.

4. The author had interviews with Lawrence Klippenstein, archivist and historian of the Heritage center at CMBC.

5. Klippenstein, 1988.

6. Interview with Gerhard Ens, editor of Der Bote, summer of 1988.

7. The author visited each of the 47 Mennonite churches in Winnipeg, and interviewed most of the pastors.

8. Kopp , "MB Churches," pp. 1-72.

CHAPTER 8

1. A count of the 1988 membership list of the Manitoba Builders Association contained thirty-six Mennonite names of businesses.

2. C.A. DeFehr, Memories of My Life (Winnipeg: C.A. DeFehr, 1967).

3. DeFehr, Memories, p. 69.

4. Interview with Arthur C. DeFehr, March 3, 1989.

5. DeFehr, Memories, p. 231.

6. Interview with A.A. DeFehr, September 9, 1988, Chairman of the Board, Palliser Furniture.

7. A.A. DeFehr, September 9.

8. Interview with A.A. DeFehr and Art DeFehr, President of Palliser, September 9, 1988 and written information received from Palliser.

9. "Leaning into the Wind: Being Christians in Business," Christian Week (March 8, 1988), pp. 10-11.

10. Interview with John Klassen, President of Monarch Industries Ltd., February 20, 1989.

11. Klassen, February 20.

12. Interview with Irene Pauls, Klassen Manufacturing Ltd., July 11, 1988.

13. Interview with A.J. Thiessen, Chairman, and Bernie Thiessen, President of Grey Goose Corporation, February 24, 1989.

14. Thiessen, February 24.

15. A.J. Thiessen, mimeographed write-up of his involvements, 1989.

16. Thiessen, February 24.

17. Interview with Gerald Reimer, Reimer Express Lines Ltd., March 1, 1989.

18. Reimer, March 1.

19. Reimer, March 1.

20. George Tatlock, "50 Years of Business Progress," in Fiftieth Anniversary of the Mennonite Settlement in North Kildonan. Ed. Karl Fast (Winnipeg: Anniversary Committee, 1978), pp. 53-54.

21. Tatlock, "50 Years," pp. 52-58.

22. Tatlock, "50 Years," pp. 54, 56.

23. Interview with Art Redekopp, February 22, 1989.

24. Interview with Bill Fast, President of Willmar Windows, February 22, 1989.

25. Fast, February 22.

26. Interview with John Rademaker, Owner and Product Marketing Director of Kitchen Craft Cabinetry, February 20, 1989.

27. Rademaker, February 20.

28. Interview with Henry Rempel, Vice President of All-Fab Building Components, February 17, 1989.

29. Interview with George Bock, Jr., Woodland Supply and Manufacturing, February 17, 1989.

30. Interview with Albert DeFehr, President of Red River Realty, February 24, 1989.

31. Interview with Martin Bergen, President of Marlborough Development Corporation, March 4, 1989.

32. Bergen, March 4.

33. Albert DeFehr, February 24, 1989.

34. Interview with Russ Loewen, Penner Foods, Winnipeg, February 17, 1989.

CHAPTER 9

1. "Annual Report, 1983-1984." Concordia Hospital, Winnipeg, 1984.

2. Interview with Siegfried Enns, Executive Director, July 18, 1988

3. "Annual Report, 1986-87," Bethania Mennonite Personal Care Home, Winnipeg, 1987, and interview with Helmut Epp, Director.

4. Telephone interview with Frank Giesbrecht, Coordinator of Sunset House, December 13, 1988.

5. Telephone interview with John Rempel, coordinator of Autumn House and Arlington House, December 13, 1988.

6. John Rempel and Frank Giesbrecht, December 13.

7. Interview with Helmuth Klassen, Administrator of Donwood Homes, July 12, 1988; "Annual Report, 1988" Mennonite Brethren Geriatric Association of Metro Winnipeg Incorporated.

8. Helmuth Klassen, July 12.

9. Helmuth Klassen, July 12.

10. Interview with John Doerksen, Director of Bethel Place, and a brochure "Presenting Bethel Place."

CHAPTER 10

1. Toews, MB History, p. 276.

2. Toews, MB History, p. 279.

3. Telephone conversations with Ron Loeppky, Registrar of Canadian Mennonite Bible College and the Registrar's Office of Mennonite Brethren Bible College, December 9, 1988.

4. The author used the University of Manitoba Student Directory of 1988 and counted all Mennonite student names listed. Not all names will necessarily be Mennonite and some who are Mennonite will have been missed because they did not have recognizable traditional Mennonite names.

5. The 1988-89 calendars of the Universities of Manitoba and Winnipeg were used to count all names which were traditional Mennonite names.

6. Telephone interview with George Epp, Director of Mennonite Studies center, December 14, 1988.

7. Catalog, 1986-88 of the Mennonite Brethren Collegiate Institute, and telephone conversation with the Registrar's Office December 13, 1988.

8. Catalog, 1988 of the Westgate Mennonite Collegiate, and telephone conversation with the Registrar's Office, December 13, 1988.

9. School handbook of the Winnipeg Mennonite Elementary School, and a telephone conversation with the principal, December 13, 1988.

CHAPTER 11

1. Toews, MB History, p. 290.

2. Toews, MB History, pp. 285-95.

3. The author interviewed a number of the people located at 1317A Portage including Wilma Derksen, Western Regional Editor of The Mennonite Reporter, and Ingrid Peters of Mediation Services.

4. Interview with Harry Loewen, Editor of the Journal of Mennonite Studies and occupant of the Chair of Mennonite Studies.

5. Interview with Dan Block, Director of MB Communications, January 25, 1989 and information sent to me.

6. Block. January 25.

7. Interview with Victor Sawatzky, Director of Faith and Life Communications, January 23, 1989.

8. Sawatzky, January 23.

CHAPTER 12

1. Wesley Berg, From Russia with Music: A Study of the Mennonite Choral Singing Tradition in Canada (Winnipeg: Hyperion Press, 1985), pp. 65-80.

2. Berg, Music, pp. 65-80.

3. Wesley Berg, Choral Festivals and Choral Workshops Among Mennonites of Manitoba and Saskatchewan, 1900-1960, Ph.D. dissertation, University of Washington, Seattle, 1979, pp. 115-8.

4. Berg, dissertation, pp. 115-8.

5. Berg, Music, p. 136.

6. Interview with Ben and Esther Horch, July 19, 1988.

7. Berg, dissertation, pp. 122-6.

8. Interview with George Wiebe, February 13, 1989.

9. Wiebe, February 13.

10. Interview with William Baerg, March 15, 1989.

11. Flyers announcing the programs to be given and interview with Henry Engbrecht, March 22, 1989.

12. Winnipeg Mennonite Children's Choir, Winnipeg, 1970, pp. 1-44.

13. Interview with John Enns, January 30, 1989.

14. Arnold Schellenberg, A Study of Acculturation Proneness of an Ethnic Subculture Within an Urban Community: Mennonite Musicians in Winnipeg. M.A. thesis, University of Manitoba, Winnipeg, 1968.

15. Interviews with Al Reimer, January 30, 1989 and Elizabeth Peters, February 9, 1989.

16. Victor G. Doerksen and Harry Loewen, eds., "Introduction," <u>Collected Works: Arnold Dyck</u>, Volume I (Winnipeg: Manitoba Historical Society, 1985), pp. 1-13.

17. Arnold Dyck, <u>Verloren in der Steppe</u>, Volumes 1-5 (North Kildonan: Regehr Printers, 1944-48).

18. Arnold Dyck, <u>Koop enn Bua</u> (North Kildonan and Steinbach, 1948-60).

19. Arnold Dyck, "Aus Meinem Leben," in <u>Collected Works: Arnold Dyck,</u> Volume I, pp. 461-513.

20. The five editors came out with the first three volumes 1985, 1986 and 1988 and two others will appear soon.

21. Al Reimer, <u>My Harp is Turned to Mourning</u> (Winnipeg: Hyperion Press, 1985). Hyperion Press also published the two Neufeld and Harder translations in 1977 and 1979.

22. Hyperion Press published most of these volumes, and CMBC Publications published <u>Fritz Senn</u>.

23. Rudy Wiebe is the best known modern Mennonite writer. Most of his novels were published by McClelland and Stewart of Toronto.

24. Patrick Friesen's volumes have been published by Turnstone Press of Winnipeg.

25. Di Brandt's volume was published by Turnstone Press of Winnipeg.

26. Published by Good Books Publishers, Intercourse, Pennsylvania.

27. Interview with John J. Enns, January 30, 1989.

28. Programs and literature put out by Winnipeg Mennonite theater, 1988.

29. Interview and letter from Marlene Neustaedter, Executive Director of Manitoba Arts Council, February 2, 1989.

30. "Annual Reports" 1983-87, Manitoba Arts Council, were examined for data.

CHAPTER 13

1. Frank Epp, <u>Partners in Service: The Story of the Mennonite Central Committee Canada</u> (Winnipeg: Mennonite Central Committee Canada, 1963).

2. Telephone discussion with Daniel Zehr, Executive Director of MCC Canada, Winnipeg, December 13, 1988.

3. Epp, <u>Partners in Service</u>, p. 22.

4. Trudy Nicolle, "Mediation Services: Pioneer and Innovator, 1979-1987." Unpublished Criminology Field Experience paper, Department of Sociology, University of Manitoba, August 5, 1987.

5. Neta Enns, <u>West End Community Self-Help Thrift and Gift Shop, 1972-1987</u> (Winnipeg: MCC Manitoba Thrift Shops, 1987), p. 1.

6. Enns, <u>MCC Thrift Shop</u>, pp. 16-17.

7. Allan Siebert, "Canadian Foodgrains Bank: A Christian Response to Hunger" (Winnipeg: Canadian Foodgrains Bank 1987), p. 3.

8. Neil Janzen, "Annual Report," Mennonite Economic Development Association, Winnipeg, 1987.

CHAPTER 14

1. Leo Driedger, "Urbanization of Mennonites in Post-War Canada," <u>Journal of Mennonite Studies,</u> Volume 6 (1988).

2. Driedger, "Urbanization," 1988.

3. The author made a special survey in 1988 of churches in 15 metropolitan centers.